New Testament
30
Interactive
Stories for Young Children

Steven James

Standard
PUBLISHING
Bringing The Word to Life

Cincinnati, Ohio

Dedication
To Brother Ray and Betty Sue

Thanks & Acknowledgments
Thanks to Trinity, Ariel, and Eden, for all of your enthusiasm, creative ideas, spontaneity,
and weirdness. This book wouldn't be what it is if it weren't for you!
Thanks to Ruth for encouraging me to write for her again,
to Tammy and Dawn for your attention to detail, to Pamela for your friendship and
continual guidance and, of course, to Liesl, for sticking with me through it all.

Published by Standard Publishing, Cincinnati, Ohio
www.standardpub.com

Printed in the United States of America

Cover design: Liz Malwitz Design
Cover illustration: Paula Becker
Interior design: Liz Malwitz Design
Editorial team: Dawn Korth, Ruth Frederick

13 12 11 10 09 08 07   5 4 3 2 1

ISBN 978-0-7847-1940-4

Table of Contents

30 New Testament Interactive Stories for Young Children

Chapter 1

The Birth of the Baby King

BASED ON: Matthew 1:18-25 and Luke 1:26-38, 2:1-7

BIG IDEA: At precisely the right moment in history, God sent his Son, our Savior, into the world. Jesus was born in a miraculous way, just as the prophets had foretold.

BACKGROUND: Throughout the centuries, God had promised his people a Savior. During the reign of King Herod, the time had come for his arrival. First an angel promised Elizabeth a special son (John the Baptist). Then her relative, Mary, received her own heavenly visitor who promised that her miraculous Son would be the Savior.

When Jesus was born, shepherds were the first ones to hear the good news. They were also the first ones to share it with others!

KEY VERSE: "But when the time had fully come, God sent his Son, born of a woman, born under law, to redeem those under law, that we might receive the full rights of sons" (Galatians 4:4, 5).

Your students may already be familiar with this story. The more familiar they are with a story, the easier it will be to act out part of the story with the children.

Because of the variety of emotions in this story, this would be a good story to use pretend masks.

Explain that you're going to do a special story in which the whole class can help you by putting on pretend masks! **"Put out your hands, kids! I'm going to give you each a box of imaginary masks! . . . Now, let's practice for this story. Whatever mask I put on, put the same mask on!"**

Pick up an imaginary mask and put it on your face. Cover your face with your hands. Then when you pull your hands away, make a huge happy face. Put your hands up to cover your face to take off the mask. Then pull your hands away and have a normal face again. After putting each mask on, remind the children, "Take it off." Then put the next mask on. Practice with a sad face, then an angry one, then a surprised face. Have fun with it.

You may also wish to make sounds as you put the masks on, like a gasp for the surprised mask, or a crying sound for the sad mask.

Then introduce the story. **"OK! Great! Let's all start out with our normal faces, without any masks on."**

Long ago, there was a woman named Mary. One day an angel appeared to her and she was really surprised! Everybody show me how <u>surprised</u> she was! *(Put on the masks together and look around at each other.)* **. . . And take it off** *(take them off)* **. . . And she was also scared! Show me how Mary looked when she was <u>scared</u> . . . Good! And take it off. . . .**

Good job! Then, when the angel told Mary that God was sending her a special baby, she was totally <u>surprised</u>! Let's put on our surprised masks . . . Good!

Then the angel told her the baby would be her Savior! And she was very happy! Let's see a <u>happy face</u>! . . . Great!

She was planning to marry a man named Joseph, and when she told him about the baby, he was <u>surprised</u> . . . and <u>sad</u> . . . because he knew he wasn't the baby's daddy. But then, in a dream, an angel told him to go ahead and get married and help raise Jesus. Of course, when the angel said that, he was <u>surprised</u> . . .

Then he told Mary that he still wanted to get married, and she was <u>happy</u> . . .

They went to Bethlehem and there, the baby was born. Mary and Joseph were very <u>happy</u> about that! . . . <u>happier</u> . . . even <u>happier</u>! . . .

Now, in the hills outside the city, some shepherds were watching some sheep to make

sure nobody hurt them. And then they saw an angel! And they were <u>surprised</u>! . . . And <u>scared</u>! . . .

The angel told them to go to Bethlehem and find a Savior wrapped in blankets and lying in a manger. So they went, and when they found Jesus, they were <u>happy</u> . . . And they told everyone they met about Jesus!

And everyone who heard about the special baby was <u>surprised</u> . . . and very, very <u>happy</u>! . . .

The end!

You could also tell this story from the perspective of one of the characters in the story. This is called a monologue. Here's an example of a monologue that retells the story from the angel's perspective. Talk in a voice that is a little bit silly and consider using a simple costume when you act like Gabriel.

Yup. You shoulda seen her face. The moment I told her she was specially chosen by God, she freaked out! Yup. That girl was scared half to death! So I just said, "Don't be freaking out, Mary! God is with you! And you're going to have a special baby who'll rule a kingdom that never ends!"

Yup. That's what I said. And then she was all confused and said, "But how will this be since I don't have a husband to give me a baby?" Yup. It was a good question. I mean babies don't just drop from trees, you know!

So I just told her that nothing is impossible with God. Yup. That's what I said. And she accepted that. Yup, she really was a woman of great faith.

Yup. I like being God's messenger all right. Especially when I get to deliver good news. Actually, I got to deliver the best news of all . . .Yup. Yup. Yup.

This story naturally has lots of sounds in it. After all, Jesus was born in a barn! This opens up the opportunity for you to include sound effects and audience participation in your story. As you tell the story with sound effects, encourage the children to join along![1]

Mary and Joseph came into the town. They were looking for a place to stay. But nobody had room! The streets were full of people! Pretend that you're getting smushed by all kinds of people . . . Good! So they went into a nearby barn to sleep.

They heard the sounds of sheep . . . Baa! Baa! And cows . . . Moo! Moo! And horses . . . Neigh! Neigh! And crickets . . . Chirp! Chirp! And maybe even roosters . . . Cock-a-doodle-doo! Cock-a-doodle-doo!

Soon, the time came for baby Jesus to be born. And when he was born, he started to do what all babies do—he cried! Pretend to cry like a little baby . . . WAAAA . . . WAAAA! . . . Good!

Now, outside of town, there were men camping. They were making sure no one hurt their sheep. Some sheep were probably sleeping . . . *Zzzzz* . . . *Zzzzz* . . . But some were probably awake! . . . Baa! Baa!

Suddenly, an angel came! The shepherds were scared! Show me how they might have looked! . . . Good!

But the angel said, "Don't be scared; your Savior is born!"

Then, more angels came! They all praised God! Let's lift our hands up like we're praising God . . . Good!

After the angels went back to Heaven, the shepherds went to the barn and found the sheep . . . Baa! Baa! . . . And cows . . . Moo! Moo! And horses . . . Neigh! Neigh! And crickets . . . Chirp! Chirp! And roosters . . . Cock-a-doodle-doo! Cock-a-doodle-doo!

And best of all, they saw the baby Jesus for themselves. Maybe he was crying . . . WAAAA . . . WAAAA! Maybe he was sleeping . . . *Zzzzz* . . . *Zzzzz*. But whatever he was doing, they knew right away he really was their Savior!

And from then on, they told everyone they met, "Jesus, the Savior has been born!" Let's say that together: "JESUS, THE SAVIOR HAS BEEN BORN!" Hurray!

Summary

The Word poured himself into a baby so small,
He was born in a stable and slept in a stall.
He was GOD wrapped in MAN
Like words wrapped in a song.
    So helplessly human, yet all-mightily strong!
    (And pleasing to God 'cause he never did wrong.
    He's the only one ever to live without sinning,
    Even though he was tempted from the very beginning!)

Our God, our Creator, was born and became
A baby called *Jesus*!
For that was his name!
Not just God
Not just Man,
Not just one or the other,
But *both* Man and God!
Both our Savior and Brother!
Both human and holy,
A guy and a God!
How strange! How amazing!
How unusually odd!
    (I'm glad he was human
    And not tuna or cod . . .)[2]

Chapter 2

The Arrival of the Wise Men

BASED ON: Matthew 2:1-12

BIG IDEA: Jesus truly is a Savior for all nations. After his birth, Gentile astronomers were more interested in finding him and worshiping him than were the Jewish religious leaders in Jerusalem.

BACKGROUND: After Jesus was born in the stable, a star appeared and a group of Magi (wise men or astronomers) from the east sought out the baby to worship him.

Many Bible scholars believe that Balaam's prophecy in Numbers 24:17 was the prophecy that led the Magi to seek Christ when the star appeared (see Matthew 2:2).

Even though the religious scholars knew about the coming Messiah, they showed no real interest in going to meet him for themselves.

KEY VERSE: "On coming to the house, they saw the child with his mother Mary, and they bowed down and worshiped him. Then they opened their treasures and presented him with gifts of gold and of incense and of myrrh" (Matthew 2:11).

It's unlikely that the wise men arrived on the night in which Jesus was born. Since Herod ordered that all the boys born in Bethlehem over the last two years be killed, and the wise men came to the house rather than the stable (see Matthew 2:11) we can guess that after Jesus was born, Mary and Joseph moved into a house in Bethlehem and it was there that the Magi visited them.

The men we refer to as the "wise men" or "Magi" were probably astrologers or astronomers from the region of modern-day Iran or Iraq.

When telling this story to young children, you'll want to be sensitive and discerning when talking about Herod's order to kill all the baby boys in Bethlehem. It might be best to avoid talking about death and simply say, "The mean king ordered that the soldiers get rid of all the baby boys!"

This story would work well for an imaginary journey. Invite the students to join along as you use creative dramatics to introduce the story.

> **Kids, let's all pretend that we are no longer in this room, but that we're riding some camels through the desert. . . . Is anyone riding a fast camel? . . . Does your camel rock back and forth as he walks? . . . Oh, boy! Let's ride our camels over the rocky path . . . Oh, no! It's so bouncy! . . .**
>
> **Now, is it hot here in the desert? . . . Whew! . . . Grab your water bottle and take a nice long drink of cool water . . . Glug, glug, glug, glug! . . . Good! Oh, look! The sun is setting! Let's climb off our camels . . . Feed your camel some food . . . Don't let it bite you!** *(Of course, when you say this, some of the kids will act like the camel bit them. That's OK. Accept it and have fun with it.)* **I said *don't* let the camel bite you! . . .** *(now all the kids will get bitten!)* **. . . Oh, well . . .**

Now, let's pull out our blankets . . . Unroll them . . . and lie down for the night. . . . It can get cold in the desert at night when the sun goes down. Brr! . . .

I wonder what kind of animals live here in the desert? . . . Are there any owls? Can you make the sound of the owls? . . . What about wolves? . . . Oh, my, it sounds like the wolves are getting closer! . . . But now, they're running far away . . .

Now, everybody look up into the sky! . . . There sure are a lot of stars! And there's a really, really bright star right over there! It's so bright and shiny, I think I need to put on my sunglasses. Put on your sunglasses, kids! . . .

Now, let's all go to sleep . . . Um, take off your sunglasses first . . .

And . . . *(snore for a few moments and then wake up)* . . .

OK! It's morning! Let's stretch . . . and pack up our blankets . . . and sunglasses . . . Climb onto your camel . . . We have to head toward that star! It's leading us toward something very important! Ride your camels . . . Fast . . . Slow . . . Bouncy . . . Smooth . . . Fast . . . Slow . . . Bouncy . . . Smooth . . .

(If desired, extend the journey by asking, "How else might the camels have moved?")

And look! The star has led us to a house! Hmm . . . I wonder who lives in this house? Let's push open the door . . . I wonder why the star would lead us here? Let's all sit down and listen to find out what's going to happen next in the story . . .

When using props to tell a story, pull them out of a special box or colorful cloth bag. Or wear an apron or a fishing vest (and perhaps bring a tackle box) and pull the props out of the many pockets or drawers.

For the following story, you may wish to wrap the props up like Christmas presents, or you could just pull each object out of the story bag or box.

Boys and girls, after Jesus was born, some men followed the light of a star *(star stickers or a candle)* just like we did a few minutes ago—and they came to the house *(a picture of a house or a doll house)* where baby Jesus was staying with Joseph *(G.I. Joe or action figure)* and Mary *(a Barbie doll)*.

Then, the wise men pulled out some presents for Jesus. The first one was *(rip open the present, or pull out the golden object)* . . . gold! The second present was *(rip open the present, or pull out the kitchen spices such as cinnamon)* . . . expensive spices! And the third was *(rip open the present, or pull out the cologne or perfume)* . . . special perfume!

Then they prayed to Jesus and worshiped him because he was their king *(a crown)*. And they went back home on their camels *(a toy horse, if desired)* with lots of joy in their hearts.

The end.

If you choose to include the wise men's visit to King Herod as you tell the story, you could also use the following additional items as you tell the story:
- small crown (King Herod)
- huge crowd (King Jesus)
- toy telescope (for seeing the star)
- apple (the teachers of the law)
- calendar (Herod asks when the star first appeared)
- bottle of Joy dishwashing liquid (the wise men see the baby and are filled with "Joy")
- map (the wise men went home a different way)

Summary

Long, long ago and far, far away
Baby Jesus was born in a stable one day.
And a star began shining in the evening sky
So some men who were waiting for that star to come by,
      Saw the star in the sky and knew it was right,
      So they followed that shining star through the night!

For days and for weeks they walked on the sand,
To find the new king who'd been born in the land.
"A new king is here!" they said as they went
      (Though they weren't sure exactly
      Why that king had been sent.)
Yet, they followed that star through the heat and the cold,
And then they found Jesus, (who wasn't too old)
      And handed him presents of spices and gold!

Then they bowed to worship the king they had found
And they climbed on their camels and turned back around
For they'd found what they searched for: the king of the Jews,
And now it was time to share the good news!

Chapter 3

Mary Finds Jesus at the Temple

BASED ON: Luke 2:41-52

BIG IDEA: Even from an early age, Jesus understood his true identity as God's Son. In this story, he reminds his mother who he truly is.

BACKGROUND: While Jesus was a baby, Mary and Joseph fled with him to Egypt to protect him from the murderous King Herod. After returning to Nazareth, they faithfully journeyed to Jerusalem each year to celebrate the Feast of the Passover.

When Jesus was twelve years old, he stayed behind at the Temple in Jerusalem and they inadvertently left for home without him. When they realized their mistake, they began to search for him and eventually found him (after three days) still in the Temple carrying on theological discussions with the rabbis.

It's noteworthy that this is the only instance on record where Mary mistakenly referred to Joseph as Jesus' father (see Luke 2:48). When she did, Jesus quickly corrected her.

KEY VERSE: "'Why were you searching for me?' he asked. 'Didn't you know I had to be in my Father's house?'" (Luke 2:49)

Many people think this story is about how Mary and Joseph searched for Jesus when he was lost. But Jesus was never lost! He knew where he was and why he was there. If only Mary had remembered who Jesus really was, she wouldn't have had to search for him. She would have known right away where he was and what he would be doing.

Repetition and simple refrains are helpful to use when telling stories to young children. The students will look forward to joining along whenever the refrain comes up in the story.

You may wish to create simple gestures for the children to do during the refrain.[3]

When Jesus was a boy, his parents took him to the worship place for a special time of praying and singing. But when the time came to go home, they couldn't find Jesus anywhere!

Where is Jesus?
Where is Jesus?
Where could he be? (repeat and invite the children to join you)

They realized Jesus was missing! So what do you think they did? . . . Right! They looked for him! They looked high! *(look up)* **. . . They looked low!** *(look down)* **. . . They looked this way!** *(look left)* **. . . They looked that way!** *(look right)* **. . . They looked all around!** *(stand up, turn in a circle looking)* **. . . But they couldn't find Jesus anywhere!**

Where is Jesus?
Where is Jesus?
Where could he be? (repeat with the children)

Boys and girls, they were getting scared that something bad might have happened! They went to their friends and looked even faster! *(Encourage the children to join you! This time do the actions faster than before)* **They looked high! . . . They looked low! . . . They looked this way! . . .**

They looked that way! . . . They looked all around! (*stand up and spin like before*) . . . But they couldn't find Jesus anywhere!

> *Where is Jesus?*
> *Where is Jesus?*
> *Where could he be?* (*repeat*)

By now, they really *were* scared! They went back to town and looked fastest of all! (*do the actions even faster!*) They looked high! . . . They looked low! . . . They looked this way! . . . They looked that way! . . . They looked all around! . . . But they couldn't find Jesus anywhere!

> *Where is Jesus?*
> *Where is Jesus?*
> *Where could he be?* (*repeat*)

Finally, after three days of looking, Mary and Joseph found Jesus sitting in the worship place! He was talking to the priests and leaders and teaching them about God!

His parents didn't know what to think! But Jesus told them, "You should have known I'd be here because God is my Father! And this is his house!"

So they went home, and Jesus obeyed his parents. He grew bigger and stronger and smarter, and even closer to God than ever before.

And even today some people might wonder,

> *Where is Jesus?*
> *Where is Jesus?*
> *Where could he be?* (*repeat*)

Where is Jesus now, kids? . . . That's right, he's in Heaven and in the hearts of all who believe in him!

The end.

As you lead the following story dramatization, invite the children to give you their ideas. Then, act out their ideas one at a time. (The following examples are provided to show you how this activity might work. When you perform the story with your class, it may be somewhat different because your students will suggest different ideas.)

If the children tell you they have found Jesus during the story, say, "Well, that looks like Jesus, but I think we need to keep looking!" Remember, try to accept whatever the children say and find a way to use their suggestions for the story. Don't correct them if they say something silly like, "They looked for Jesus on the moon!" Say, "Right! They did!" Then act it out and after the activity is finished you can ask the kids, "OK, we acted out some silly things! Did they really look for Jesus on the moon? Of course not! But they did look in the city and among their friends and with the group of people traveling back to Bethlehem. We know that because the Bible tells us so!"

Boys and girls, Jesus went to worship God with his mother and with Joseph, her husband. Then, when Mary and Joseph left to bring Jesus back home, they thought he was with the other people in their group. But he wasn't!

When Jesus' mommy realized he was missing, how do you think she felt? . . . That's right! And then she began to look all over for Jesus! Let's pretend that we are looking for Jesus just like she did! Where's the first place you think we should look? . . .

Great! Let's look in the crowd of people . . . It's really crowded here . . . Stand up tall and stretch up high to look over everyone's head . . . Now get low and look between their legs! . . . Look under your toes. Is he underneath your feet? Nope, Jesus isn't here anywhere. Where else might he be? *(allow them to respond)* . . .

OK, let's look at the park! Climb up the slide . . . And look around . . . Do you see Jesus? . . . No? . . . Well, let's slide down the slide and go look in the sandbox! WHEE! . . . OK, push the sand away. . . . Is Jesus buried up to his neck in the sand? . . . Hmm . . . Where else can we look?

Great! Let's go to the city! . . . Watch out for people riding camels! . . . Don't let the camels bump into you! . . . Ouch! . . .

(Whatever else your children suggest, end by searching at the temple.)

Hmm . . . Let's look in one more place. Let's look at the temple! Push open the door . . . Step inside, and—oh, my! . . . What's that I hear? . . . It's someone teaching God's Word . . . Let's hurry through the temple! But I guess we shouldn't run in here, let's just walk fast . . . Good . . . It sounds like that's Jesus talking! We found him! There he is! . . . Run up to Jesus . . . Give him a big hug; you missed him so much! . . .

OK, everyone! Sit down! I'm going to read a poem about this story to help us all remember it even better!

Summary

Mary was searching! Oh, where was her son?
Could Jesus be hiding or off having fun?
Then Joseph went with her to search high and low.
Oh, where was that boy? Oh, where did he go?
      They looked by the camels. They looked by the fence.
      They looked by the donkeys. And inside the tents!
They searched in the city. They searched in the town!
They looked high and low and they looked all around—
By the road and the trees and then out by the brook;
      But they couldn't find Jesus wherever they looked!

Then they went to the temple when the day was all through
      (Neither Joseph nor Mary knew what else to do.)
And when they walked in, to their shock and surprise,
They saw Jesus was teaching all the men who were wise!
He was asking them questions and explaining God's Word
And the men were amazed at the things that they heard!

"Where were you, my son!" his mother declared.
But Jesus just said, "Mother, why were you scared?
Why were you searching and why were you sad?
I had to be here, with my heavenly Dad!
For his work is my work, and I thought you would know
That I must do his work wherever I go!"

Well, his mother and Joseph didn't know what to say,
For they still didn't know why he'd stayed there that day.
But they took him back home where he listened and prayed.
And whatever they told him, Jesus always obeyed.

Chapter 4

Jesus Refuses to Sin in the Wilderness

BASED ON: Mark 1:12, 13 and Luke 4:1-13

BIG IDEA: Jesus withstood Satan's temptations by turning to God's Word. We can learn from Jesus' example to turn to God's Word whenever we're tempted today.

BACKGROUND: Immediately after Jesus' baptism, the Holy Spirit led him into the desert to be tempted by the devil. The point of the temptations wasn't to lead Jesus into sin, but rather to strengthen his faith and harden his resolve to follow God's will. Despite Satan's persistence, Jesus never once gave in to sin.

KEY VERSE: "Jesus answered, 'It says: "Do not put the Lord your God to the test."' When the devil had finished all this tempting, he left him until an opportune time" (Luke 4:12, 13).

If you compare Matthew 4:1-11 and Luke 4:1-13 you'll notice that Matthew records the devil's temptations in a slightly different order than Luke does. The order of the temptations isn't as important as the goal of the temptations: to disrupt God's plan and thwart God's desire to save people through his sinless Son, Jesus.

Since this story is mostly a conversation between Jesus and the devil, it would work well to do as a skit. Stories with lots of dialogue are harder to act out as a class because they have fewer actions. However, they are often easier to change into scripts in which two people carry on a conversation.

If desired, wrap a rubber snake around Satan's neck and let Jesus wear a crown, or choose another simple costume piece for them to wear. Photocopy the script and rehearse together before class.

SATAN: *(To the children)* **Hee, hee, hee!**
You wait and see!
I'll make Jesus do something wrong!
And I'll get him to do it before very long!

(Enter Jesus)

SATAN: *(To Jesus)* **Hi, Jesus.**

JESUS: **Hi, Satan.**

SATAN: **You look hungry.**

JESUS: **I am. I haven't eaten anything in almost six weeks!**

SATAN: **Well, that's silly! Go ahead and turn some of those rocks over there into bread before you die of hunger!**

JESUS: **No, Satan, no! Go far away!**
Don't try to make me sin today!

I'm trusting in God and not in you!
So I'll only do what he tells me to.
And he wants me to rely more on him than on food. It says so in the Bible!

SATAN: *(To the children)* Hee, hee, hee!
                You wait and see!
                I'll make Jesus do something wrong!
                And I'll get him to do it before very long!

SATAN: *(To Jesus)* Come with me, Jesus.

JESUS: OK.

(Walk to the other side of the stage)

SATAN: *(Gesturing)* Look at all the riches and power and pleasures of the world! I'll give
                them all to you if you'll just worship me!

JESUS: No, Satan, no! Go far away!
                Don't try to make me sin today!
                I'm trusting in God and not in you!
                So I'll only do what he tells me to.
                We should only worship God and no one else! It says so in the Bible!

SATAN: *(To the children)* Hee, hee, hee!
                You wait and see!
                I'll make Jesus do something wrong!
                And I'll get him to do it before very long!

SATAN: *(To Jesus)* Well then, if God loves you so much he'll protect you! Jump off the
                temple *(point to the temple, or step up onto a chair or table)* and *(sarcastically)* he'll send
                his angels to save you. It says so in the Bible, right?

JESUS: No, Satan, no! Go far away!
                Don't try to make me sin today!
                I'm trusting in God and not in you!
                So I'll only do what he tells me to.
                We shouldn't try to make God prove he's there! It says so in the Bible!

SATAN: *(To the children)* Rats and phooey and curses too,
                I wish he'd do what I tell him to!
                But I'll tempt him more again someday,
                And I know I'll get him to disobey!

JESUS: *(To the children)* Don't worry kids, I will NOT disobey.
                I'll always do things my Father's way!

(Satan and Jesus bow and exit)

For the following story, invite the children to sing each refrain with you to the tune of "Here We Go 'Round the Mulberry Bush." As you sing the refrains, have the children join you by doing the suggested actions.

Practice the story a couple of times before class to make sure you're familiar with the refrains and the actions.

WHAT TO SAY:	SUGGESTED REFRAIN:	SUGGESTED ACTIONS:
When Jesus was ready to start telling people about God, he went into the desert.	Jesus went in to the wilderness, The wilderness, The wilderness. Jesus went in to the wilderness. So early in the morning. *(repeat with the children)*	Walk in place.
While Jesus was in the desert, he didn't eat any food for almost six weeks!	Jesus did not eat up any food, Any food, Any food. Jesus did not eat up any food. So early in the morning. *(repeat)*	Shake your head "no."
While Jesus was there, the devil tried to trick him into disobeying God!	Oh, the devil tried to get him to sin, [To] get him to sin, [To] get him to sin. The devil tried to get him to sin, So early in the morning. *(repeat)*	Act sneaky.
But Jesus told him, "No!" and Jesus showed him where the Bible says we should obey God and not the devil.	Jesus continued to trust in God, Trust in God, Trust in God. Jesus continued to trust in God. So early in the morning. *(repeat)*	Fold hands as if you're praying.
The devil tried to trick Jesus three times, but finally he went away because he saw Jesus was not going to disobey God.	So finally the devil went far away, Far away, Far away. Finally the devil went far away, So early in the morning. *(repeat)*	Wave goodbye.
Jesus showed us what to do when we're tempted: WE SHOULD OBEY THE BIBLE AND TRUST IN GOD JUST LIKE JESUS DID!	Jesus taught us to trust God's Word, Trust God's Word, Trust God's Word. Jesus taught us to trust God's Word, EVERY SINGLE MORNING! *(repeat)*	Hold your hands out like you're holding a Bible.
The end! Let's hear a cheer for Jesus!		

Summary

The devil was sneaky. The devil was mean.
So when Jesus was hungry, he came on the scene.
And he tried to get Jesus to do what was bad!
But Jesus would never dishonor his Dad!

The devil said, "Jesus, you're hungry I know,
You could turn all those rocks into freshly baked dough!"
But the hunger he had didn't need to be fixed,
He trusted in God,
        Not food
                And not tricks!

Then the devil showed him riches and offered him power,
If only he'd worship the devil that hour.
But Jesus said, "Devil, why do you bother?
I won't worship you, I only pray to my Father!"

"Jump off of the temple!" said the devil, "Because
God says he'll protect you—let's see what he does!"
But Jesus said, "Testing the Father isn't right,
He doesn't have to show us his power or might!"

So when the devil realized Jesus wouldn't give in
And that he couldn't be tempted to be naughty or sin,
He went far away. And Jesus passed the test.
And angels came from Heaven and helped Jesus rest.

Chapter 5

Jesus Asks People to Become His Followers

BASED ON: Matthew 4:18-22; 9:9-13

BIG IDEA: Jesus invited different people to become his followers. Often they had to leave their old lives behind when they chose to be with Jesus.

BACKGROUND: As Jesus began his preaching ministry, he called a group of men to be his close followers, or disciples (sometimes called "apostles"). The first disciples were four fishermen—two sets of brothers: James and John, and Peter and Andrew. Jesus also called a tax collector named Matthew (or Levi) to be one of his followers.

Before making a final decision about which twelve men to appoint to be his apostles, Jesus carefully prayed about his decision (see Luke 6:12-16).

KEY VERSE: "Going on from there, he saw two other brothers, James son of Zebedee and his brother John. They were in a boat with their father Zebedee, preparing their nets. Jesus called them, and immediately they left the boat and their father and followed him" (Matthew 4:21, 22).

Jesus first invited a group of fishermen to follow him; then we hear him invite Matthew, a tax collector. When these men followed Jesus, they had to reprioritize their lives and leave behind their families and their means of support. Today we may not have to leave our families, town, or jobs when we become Christians, but following Jesus will always create a new and transformed life—both in big ways and small.

If children don't know what a tax collector does, explain that he had to collect money from the people to give to the leaders in the land—but sometimes he probably took more than he was supposed to, just to make himself rich! However, Jesus loved everyone, including tax collectors.

For this first activity, invite the children to chant and do the actions with you.

Boys and girls, the first followers of Jesus were fishermen. They would throw big nets into the water and try to catch fish in the nets. Let's pretend we're fishermen and women and boys and girls! First we have to get the nets ready to go fishing. So . . .

(with rhythm)
Spread your nets! *(Spread out your nets)*
Spread your nets!
Spread your nets out wide today!
(Repeat, and invite the children to chant with you)

Scrub your nets! *(Scrub the nets)*
Scrub your nets!
Scrub your nets so clean today!
(Repeat)

Fix your nets! *(Sew the nets)*

Fix your nets!
Fix your broken nets today!
(Repeat)

Row your boat! *(Row your boat)*
Row your boat!
Row your boat in the lake today!
(Repeat)

Drop your nets! *(Throw the nets into the water)*
Drop your nets!
Drop your nets in the sea today!
(Repeat)

Pull your nets! *(Pull the nets in)*
Pull your nets!
Pull your nets to the boat today!
(Repeat)

Did you catch any fish today, kids? . . . Show me the fish you caught! Hold 'em up! . . . I wonder if anyone caught some really big fish? . . . Are they flopping all around? . . . Are they getting all over the boat? . . . Oh, no!
Kids, we'd better row to shore before the fish flop back into the water!

(faster)
Row your boat! *(Row your boat)*
Row your boat!
Row your boat to the shore today!
(Repeat)

Look, kids! It's Jesus walking toward us on the shore! He's got some other men with him. It looks like they're following him! They want to be his friends and helpers!
Kids, he's calling to us!
Let's follow Jesus!

I hear Jesus! *(Cup your hand behind your ear)*
I hear Jesus!
I hear Jesus call today!
(Repeat)

Leave your nets! *(Throw the nets onto the ground and then wave goodbye to them)*
Leave your nets!
Leave your nets on the shore today!
(Repeat)

Follow Jesus! *(Walk in place)*
Follow Jesus!
Follow Jesus in your life today!
(Repeat)

Cheer for Jesus! *(Wave your arms high and cheer)*

Cheer for Jesus!
Cheer for Jesus! Hip, hip hooray!
(Repeat)

After doing the interactive story, have the children sit down. Then summarize some of the accounts of Jesus calling his disciples. You might wish to use the following ideas:

Kids, when Jesus was ready to start traveling around and telling people about God's love, he wanted to have some helpers. These had to be special people! So Jesus invited people to come and follow him. "Follow me!" he called. What did he say? . . . Right!

Sometimes they did, but sometimes when Jesus invited people to come, they made up excuses like, "I'm too busy," or "I have other stuff to do" or "I don't really want to put you first in my life." Now kids, were those very good reasons? . . . No they weren't!

Now the first people Jesus asked to be his followers were fishermen. And when he called to them, they left their nets and they left their families and they left their boats and sometimes they even left nets full of fish to follow Jesus!

Then a little later, Jesus went up to a rich man named Matthew who collected money from the people. Matthew gave the money to the leaders in the land. But sometimes he probably took more than he should have just so he could get rich!

Well, when Jesus called to Matthew, he stood up right away and started following Jesus. Then he threw a big party in honor of Jesus so he could invite his friends to meet Jesus too!

Below is one way you could reenact Matthew's decision to follow Jesus with his life.

OK everyone, pretend that you're carrying bags full of money . . . The bags are heavy because you have lots of money! . . . Hold out your hand for someone to give you even more money! . . .

Now, look! Here comes Jesus! . . . Let's stand up . . . and wave goodbye to all that money . . . Bye-bye money! . . . and let's follow Jesus. He has something even better than money to offer us—God's love! *(walk in place)*

Then Matthew threw a great big party for Jesus! . . . What did they do at the party? . . . *(as your children suggest ideas, act them out)* **. . . Did they run around playing games? Show me what that looked like! . . . Did they eat lots of yummy food? . . . Did they drink fresh grape juice? . . . Were they happy at the party? How happy were they? . . .**

Yes, Matthew's friends were happy to be with Jesus! But then, some people who didn't like Jesus came to the party! They were mean! Show me how those mean people looked . . .

They didn't like Matthew's friends, and they didn't think Jesus should be at a party with them. Was that a very kind way to act? . . . No it wasn't!

So Jesus told them he came to help Matthew's friends because he loved them! Matthew and his friends were happy to hear that . . . I'll bet they played some more games . . . and ate some more yummy food . . . and drank some more juice! . . .

Then Jesus told the people that he didn't come to earth to help folks who think they're fine, but to help those who know they've made mistakes! And when Jesus said all that, Matthew's friends were even happier than before . . . Even happier . . . Even happier than that! . . . because they knew Jesus had come to help them!

The end.

If your class is large enough and you have adults (or teens) to help lead each group, you could have three groups of students—one group to say/sing each refrain on page 21. Do them as a round! Otherwise, you could chant the refrains together as a large group.

If you wish, hand out maracas or other simple rhythm instruments for the children to play as you chant the words! Make up fun gestures to do for each verse!

> **Walkin' on the seashore,**
> **Steppin' on the sand.**
> **Watchin' all the waves,**
> **Washin' up on the land.**
> *(repeat)*
>
> **Sittin' at the table,**
> **Gettin' all the gold.**
> **Put it in your pocket,**
> **More than you can hold!**
> *(repeat)*
>
> **Listenin' to Jesus**
> **Callin' out to you.**
> **Askin' you to follow**
> **Whatcha gonna do?**
> *(repeat)*

Summary

Follow me!
     Follow me!
That's what he said.
Follow me!
     Follow me!
He said to the men.
So they left all their fishes.
They left all their nets.
They left all their families,
And even their pets!
They left all their riches.
They left all their stuff.
And they went off with Jesus,
For he was enough.

Yes, they went off with Jesus
To learn and to grow,
And to follow wherever
Their Savior would go!
And even today,
Jesus still calls his friends.
He helps and he teaches
[And] his love he extends,
To all who will follow,
He helps us to grow.
Yes, Jesus will lead you
Wherever you go!

Chapter 6

A Woman Meets Jesus at the Well

BASED ON:	John 4:1-42
BIG IDEA:	Jesus loves all people—men and women, boys and girls from every culture. And he offers them all new life when they come to him.
BACKGROUND:	Jesus broke down the social constraints of his day by valuing women, and in this story, by accepting a Samaritan woman. (Most Jews and Samaritans held deep prejudices against each other.) Jesus appealed to her spiritual thirst, and by the end of their conversation, she believed in him. She immediately spread the news about Jesus and, as a result, many people came to faith.
KEY VERSE:	"Many of the Samaritans from that town believed in him because of the woman's testimony, 'He told me everything I ever did.' So when the Samaritans came to him, they urged him to stay with them, and he stayed two days. And because of his words many more became believers" (John 4:39-41).

Your students may not know that Jews and Samaritans didn't like each other very much and rarely talked to each other. They lived in different places, wore different clothes, and worshiped God differently. But Jesus didn't care about all that. He loved the people from Samaria as much as he loved the Jewish people.

It's significant to note that John 4:4 says that Jesus "had to go through Samaria." Most Jews would have avoided going through there at all costs. But Jesus had to go there not only for the woman's sake, but for the sake of his disciples who needed to learn that God's love is for everyone regardless of race, background, or tradition.

For the following story, invite another teacher to help you by leading the actions and the sounds after you say the words. If you wish, only include either the suggested actions or sound effects for the story rather than both.

Invite the children to do the actions and sound effects too.

WHAT TO SAY:	SUGGESTED ACTIONS:	SUGGESTED SOUND EFFECTS:
One day Jesus and his friends were walking along the road	Walk in place.	Clippity clop. Clippity clop. *(repeat with the children)*
They were wearing sandals.	Keep walking.	Flippity flop. Flippity flop. *(repeat)*
It was hot.	Wipe your brow.	Whew! *(etc.)*
They were hungry . . .	Rub your tummy.	Grumble, grumble. Tummy grumble.
And thirsty.	Pant.	I could use some lemonade!
So Jesus sent his friends into town to get some food.	Rub your tummy.	Yummy, yummy To my tummy!
And he met a woman at the well. She was getting some water.	Hold a cup.	Splishy, splashy. Splishy, splashy. Water in my cup!

Jesus asked her for a drink	Hold out your hand.	Pretty please with sugar on top?
But she didn't want to give it to him because he was a Jew!	Hands on your hips, shake your head "no."	No way, José!
Then he told her about living water and she was surprised!	Be surprised.	Huh? What is that all about?
Of course, he meant trusting in him!	Hands over your heart.	Splishy, splashy. Splishy, splashy. Water in my HEART!
Now, this woman had some secrets she didn't think anyone else knew about!	Put your finger to your lips.	Shh! Don't say a word!
But Jesus knew about them	Be surprised.	Huh? What is that all about?
And he told her so!	Be even more surprised.	Whoa, dude! That's really weird!
So, she ran back to town to tell her friends that Jesus came from God	Run in place.	Clippity clop. Clippity clop.
She was wearing sandals.	Keep running.	Oh. Flippity flop. Flippity flop.
Meanwhile, friends came back with the food	Walk in place.	Clippity clop. Clippity clop.
They were wearing sandals too!	Keep walking.	Flippity flop. Flippity flop.
And they were surprised Jesus had been talking to a woman	Be surprised.	Huh? What is that all about?
And even more surprised because she was from a country of people they didn't like!	Be even more surprised.	Whoa, dude! That's really weird!
Then the woman came back *(do these next few lines quickly)*	Walk in place.	Clippity clop. Clippity clop.
With her friends	Faster walking	Clippity clop. Clippity clop.
They were all wearing sandals	Keep walking.	Flippity flop. Flippity flop.
They ate the food.	Pretend to eat.	Yummy, yummy To my tummy!
And drank the water.	Hold a cup.	Splishy, splashy. Splishy, splashy. Water in my cup!
And many people believed in Jesus!	Hands over your heart.	Splishy, splashy. Splishy, splashy. Water in my HEART!
Yes, Jesus loves all people	Hug yourself.	Aw
Boys,	Flex your muscles.	Yeah!
And girls,	Look pretty.	Mm
And men,	Flex even more.	YEAH!
And women,	Look even prettier.	MMMmmm
From every country in the world.	Sweep your hands out.	Whoa!
And he wants them all to drink living water—which means believing in Jesus!	Hands over your heart.	Splishy, splashy. Splishy, splashy. Water in my HEART!
The end.	Bow to the audience.	

Here's one more way to retell this story with a simple refrain. Teach the children to alternate saying, "Cool!" or "Bummer!" as you tell the story. You might also wish to use two thumbs up and two thumbs down.

STORY:	REFRAINS:
Jesus was out walking with his friends.	Cool!
They were very hungry!	Bummer.
So he sent them to town to get some food.	Cool!
But Jesus waited by the road and he was really thirsty!	Bummer.
So he walked up to the well.	Cool!
But he didn't have a bucket!	Bummer.
A woman was there getting water from the well.	Cool!
Jesus asked her to share some water, but she didn't want to!	Bummer.
Then Jesus told her he had special water that you can drink and then never get thirsty again!	Cool!
But she didn't understand what he meant!	Bummer.
Then Jesus told her about secrets from her life!	Cool!
And she knew he was from God, but she still didn't know he was the Savior!	Bummer.
Then Jesus told her he was the Savior!	Cool!
Then the disciples returned and didn't think Jesus should have been talking to that woman!	Bummer.
But she ran to town to tell her friends that she had met the Savior!	Cool!
But the disciples wanted to go home because they didn't really like the people from that country.	Bummer.
But the people believed the woman's story about Jesus!	Cool!
They came and met Jesus for themselves! *(If they say "Bummer!" Say, "No actually that was "Cool!")*	Cool!
And many people believed in Jesus from that land!	COOL!
The end!	

Summary

Jesus for foreigners! Jesus for Jews!
Jesus for everyone! That is the news!
Jesus gives water that flows from inside!
He refreshes your soul and he cleanses your pride!

The day was dry and the day was hot
When Jesus came to a special spot.
A woman was getting some water to use
But she didn't say "hi!" 'cause she didn't like Jews!

Jesus said, "May I have a little water to drink?"
But the woman didn't really know what to think.
She was just so surprised when Jesus spoke
For she didn't often talk to the Jewish folk.

But when he showed her he knew the secrets she had,
She thought, "He's from God!" and that made her glad!
Then he told her he offered fresh water for souls,
        Not water you pour into cups or in bowls.

She ran off and told all her friends, "He's the one!
He came down from Heaven! He's really God's Son!"
And many believed when they heard what he'd done
And that he knew the secrets she hadn't told anyone.

Yes, Jesus for foreigners! Jesus for Jews!
Jesus for everyone! That is the news!
Jesus gives water that flows from inside!
He refreshes your soul and he cleanses your pride!

Chapter 7

Jesus Welcomes the Children

BASED ON: Matthew 18:1-6, 10-14; 19:13-15

BIG IDEA: Jesus loves children. Adults must learn childlike humility and faith in order to enter God's kingdom.

BACKGROUND: Jesus was a popular rabbi. He taught as one with authority, yet he always exhibited genuine compassion. Parents naturally thought he was the right kind of man to bless their children, so they brought their children to Jesus.

     When the disciples tried to stop the parents, Jesus rebuked them. He explained that children don't need to become more like adults to enter the kingdom of Heaven, but rather adults need to become more childlike!

KEY VERSE: "Jesus said, 'Let the little children come to me, and do not hinder them, for the kingdom of heaven belongs to such as these.' When he had placed his hands on them, he went on from there" (Matthew 19:14, 15).

It's important for your children to know that not only did Jesus welcome the children, he said that children possess special characteristics that grown-ups need to learn (see Matthew 18:4 and Mark 10:15)! Usually, children end up feeling they need to learn stuff from their parents; while that is true, parents need to learn humility and trust from children. After all, it's only the childlike and not the childish who are welcomed into God's kingdom.

Jesus was teaching the crowds, and they were happy to listen to him. I wonder if you can show me how happy they were . . . Good! They sat quietly and listened to him when he taught. Show me how quietly they sat and how well they listened . . . Good job!

Then some of the parents brought their children to Jesus so he could bless them. The kids were excited. OK, now you get to be excited kids! . . . They were jumping up and down! . . . Some were maybe running around in circles . . . And others were acting all weird and stuff! . . .

Some of the mommies and daddies carried their kids to Jesus! OK, now let's pretend to be a grown-up carrying a kid . . . Some of the kids were heavy . . . Wow, those were some really big kids! . . .

But the disciples stood in the way, blocking them from Jesus! . . . Show me how those disciples stood! . . . They weren't happy that the parents were bringing their children to Jesus. The disciples shook their heads "no." . . . They wouldn't let the parents through! That made the parents sad . . . and the kids sad . . . But it made Jesus angry! . . .

He gathered the kids around him and hugged them! Give someone a big hug . . . And he told the disciples to become more like the kids because the kids were humble and believed in Jesus. And I also think they were excited! . . . And jumping up and down! . . . And running around in circles . . . And even acting all weird and stuff! . . .

Then, the parents carried their kids back home . . . Some of those kids were heavy . . . And the crowds of people were happy to see that Jesus loves kids. How happy were they? . . . Good!

And when the kids realized how much Jesus loved them, they were even more excited!

. . . and jumping! . . . and running . . . and acting more and more weird and stuff! . . .
But mostly, the kids were happy because they knew they mattered to Jesus . . .
The end!

Sing the following refrains to the tune of "Are You Sleeping?"

Yes, the parents wanted to bring their kids to meet Jesus . . .

Are you busy?
Are you busy?
Jesus Christ!
Jesus Christ!
Children want to meet you,
Children want to meet you,
Because you're nice.
Because you're nice.
(repeat)

But the disciples didn't want to let them through!

He's too busy!
He's too busy!
Go away.
Go away.
Jesus cannot meet you,
Jesus cannot meet you,
Here today.
Here today.
(repeat)

When Jesus saw that, he was not happy! Instead, he told them all,

I'm not busy!
I'm not busy!
Please come here!
Please come here!
I love all the children,
I love all the children,
Far and near!
Far and near!
(repeat)

Let's hear a cheer for Jesus!

Summary

Jesus was famous for the things that he'd done
For he healed all the people and helped everyone.
And they loved how he led them. They loved how he taught.
And they loved all the stories of Heaven he brought!

And Jesus welcomed children. He loved all the kids.
And he wasn't annoyed by the things that they did!
So all of the fathers, and all of the mothers
Brought children to see him. Both sisters and brothers,
Both the little and big, both the chubby and tall
Both daughters and sons, parents carried them all.

They came to meet Jesus; those girls and boys;
Laughing and giggling, and making such noise.
But all the disciples just stood in the way!
And they told them, "I'm sorry; he's busy today!"
        Then they told all those parents to please go away!

But Jesus was angry when he heard what they did!
'Cause Jesus loves parents and Jesus loves kids!
        So he said, "Bring the children. Don't get in the way!
        I want to bless all of the children today!"

Chapter 8

Jesus Arrives in Jerusalem

BASED ON: Matthew 21:1-11; Mark 11:1-11; Luke 19:28-44; and John 12:12-19

BIG IDEA: Jesus arrived in Jerusalem to an outpouring of public support. The people recognized him as the long-awaited deliverer of the Jews. Yet, knowing their hearts, Jesus couldn't share in their joy.

BACKGROUND: The crowds in Jerusalem had heard about Jesus raising Lazarus from the dead and about the other wonderful miracles he'd done. So, when Jesus arrived at the beginning of the Passover celebration, the people recognized him as a king in David's lineage and they rushed to meet him.

The Jews were looking for an earthly king and deliverer, but Jesus had a different type of kingdom to establish (see John 18:36). He even burst into tears as he thought of Jerusalem's spiritual rejection of God (see Luke 19:41-44).

KEY VERSE: "The crowds that went ahead of him and those that followed shouted,
'Hosanna to the Son of David!',
'Blessed is he who comes in the name of the Lord!',
'Hosanna in the highest!'" (Matthew 21:9).

Each of the gospel writers emphasizes different aspects of the arrival of Jesus in Jerusalem. For example, Matthew mentions that both a donkey and a colt were present while the other Gospel accounts only mention one or the other. Before you tell today's story, take a few minutes to read through each of the accounts so that you're familiar with each version of the story.

This would be a great lesson to use props with, if you can find palm branches for the children to wave! Since many modern Bible translations translate the shouting of the people differently, (for example, some say "Hosanna!" and others say "Praise God!"), choose the translation that's most appropriate for your class and then use those phrases consistently throughout the lesson.

WHAT TO SAY:	WHAT TO DO:
Long ago Jesus rode into the city. He was riding on a donkey!	Ride your donkeys! "Yee-haw!"
And everyone in the city was excited!	Excited faces and big smiles!
The people ran out to meet him!	Run in place.
They waved palm branches high in the air!	Wave your branches.
And put their coats on the ground in front of the donkey!	Put your coats on the ground.
People all over the city were singing and praising God, saying, "Hosanna!" Can you say, "Hosanna?" It means, "Praise God! Praise God!"	Shout, "Hoorah! He's here! Come on outside! Praise God! The new king has arrived!"
But some people didn't know who Jesus was!	Look confused.

They asked who he was and everyone else shouted, "Jesus the prophet from Nazareth!" (A prophet is a person who listens to God and then tells people God's Word.) Let's pretend I'm one of those people who didn't know who Jesus is. I'll say, "Who is this guy?" And you yell, all together, "JESUS THE PROPHET FROM NAZARETH!"

Let's try it. "Who is this guy?" *(allow them to respond)* . . .
I couldn't hear you. I said, "Who is this guy? . . ."
What? . . .
Oh. He must be Jesus the prophet from Nazareth!

But kids, I have to tell you—some men were angry!	Angry faces.
They scolded Jesus. "Stop them from singing!" they said,	Shake your scoldy fingers.
But Jesus only shook his head.	Smile and shake your heads.
Then he told them, "If I stop them, the rocks will cheer that I am here!"	Cheer for Jesus!
Because, kids, who is this guy? . . . What? . . . I can't hear you! . . . Oh. He must be Jesus the prophet from Nazareth!	
The end!	Bow and take a seat.

Explain that the religious leaders didn't think Jesus was God, so they didn't want people worshiping him. Jesus told them that if the people didn't shout his praises, the rest of creation would!

After telling the story to your students, invite them to act out parts of the story with you. This is an easy story to remember and to act out because the people greeting Jesus do three things: (1) they wave palm branches, (2) they take off their coats, and (3) they shout and sing to God.

OK, kids, let's pretend that we are those people welcoming Jesus to our town! First of all, they waved palm branches to meet Jesus. OK, everyone, pick up your branch . . . Good. See how heavy it is or how light it is . . . OK, now:

(with rhythm)
Wave 'em high! . . . *(act this out)*
Wave 'em high!
Wave 'em high up to the sky!
Wave 'em low!
Wave 'em low!
Wave 'em low down by your toe!
Wave 'em in the middle!
Wave 'em in the middle!
Give your bellybutton a little bitty tickle!
(Repeat)

Good job, kids! Now set them down in front of Jesus' donkey! . . . OK, let's take off our coats and lay them down before the donkey, too!

I'm takin' off my coat . . . *(act this out)*
I'm layin' it down . . .
So the donkey won't have to walk on the ground!
(Repeat)

Finally, the people sang because they were so happy to see Jesus!

"Hosanna! It's Jesus! Hosanna!" they cried.
"Hosanna! The kingdom of God has arrived!"
(Repeat several times, getting louder each time)

Luke records that as Jesus rode into the city and thought about Jerusalem's rejection of God's plan, he started to cry. Even on this great celebratory day, Jesus' compassion is evident. Use the following ideas if you want to cover that aspect of the story.

When Jesus came into the city, his friends were very happy. Show me <u>how happy they were</u> . . . Good! And some of the people were excited to see him! Show me <u>how those excited people looked</u> . . . Right! They shouted and praised God. And that made Jesus happy . . . But it made some of the people <u>mad</u> . . . Because they didn't like Jesus! Other people were <u>confused</u> . . . Because they didn't really know who Jesus was!

Then, as Jesus rode into town, he started thinking about all the people there who didn't accept God's love. And that made Jesus <u>sad</u> . . . So sad, in fact, that <u>he started to cry</u> . . .

But all the people who loved Jesus were <u>very, very happy that Jesus had come to town!</u> The end.

If desired, review the story with the children: **"Why did Jesus cry on this happy day? Do you think he would cry if he came to our town? Why? (or why not?)"**

Summary

The city was busy.
The city was packed.
Then Jesus came riding
On a donkey's back.

The people were shouting!
The shouting was loud!
They waved palm branches
Above the crowd!

And then they were singing
Laying coats on the ground.
And they shouted to God—
With a joyful sound!

      "He's coming! He's coming!
      Let the cheering begin!
      Praise God and Hosanna—
      The king has come in!"

Chapter 9

Judas Betrays Jesus in the Garden of Gethsemane

BASED ON: Matthew 26:36-56 and Mark 14:32-52

BIG IDEA: When Jesus needed his friends the most, they fell asleep, betrayed him, or ran away. Yet Jesus continued walking step by step to the cross because he knew it was God's will.

BACKGROUND: After the Last Supper, Jesus and his disciples crossed the Kidron Valley to an area known as the Garden of Gethsemane. Apparently this was a favorite place of prayer for Jesus and his disciples. Once there, Jesus prayed and submitted himself to God's plan.

Judas followed his own agenda and betrayed Jesus. The other disciples fell asleep and then ran off, leaving Jesus all alone with his enemies. The next day Jesus was unjustly sentenced to death.

KEY VERSE: "'Abba, Father,' he said, 'everything is possible for you. Take this cup from me. Yet not what I will, but what you will'" (Mark 14:36).

The death of Jesus is a very serious and intense lesson. With younger children, you may wish to avoid talking too much about his death and simply mention it in the next lesson when you talk about Easter. I'm not suggesting you don't teach the children that Jesus died for their sins, just that you avoid going into detail about the frightening and raw realities of his suffering and crucifixion.

I've included ideas in this lesson that focus on Judas's betrayal, and then a few thoughts on telling the story of Jesus' crucifixion.

For the following story, invite the children to join you as you walk with Jesus and his disciples to the Garden of Gethsemane. Consider turning off the classroom lights and using candles to create a nighttime atmosphere.

It was a dark night. Jesus and his friends were walking to a place called the Garden of Gethsemane. They wanted to go there to pray.

Let's pretend that we're walking with them through the night . . . OK, everyone. Let's walk . . . *(walk in place)*

What kind of sounds do you think we might hear walking through the nighttime? Are there any owls? . . . Whoo! Whoo! . . . What about crickets? . . . Chirp! Chirp! . . . What other sounds might we hear? . . . *(allow them to respond, then act out their ideas)*

Now this garden has lots of trees in it. Push the tree branches out of the way . . . Good! Watch where you step so you don't trip over a root . . . Look, we've come to a little meadow and Jesus is going off to pray by himself.

Now, I'll pretend to be Jesus and you be his friends. Jesus said, "I know that you're sleepy, but please stay awake." And his friends said, "We promise you, Jesus! We'll do what it takes!" Let's say your part, ready? "WE PROMISE YOU, JESUS! WE'LL DO WHAT IT TAKES!"

Good!

(JESUS PRAYS THE FIRST TIME)

OK, after I say Jesus' part, you'll say his friends' part. Jesus went off to pray and his friends fell fast asleep. OK, go to sleep everyone . . . lie down . . . Then Jesus came back and he found them all sleeping!

And they sat up . . . and yawned . . . and he said, "I know that you're sleepy, but please stay awake." And they said, ready? "WE PROMISE YOU, JESUS! WE'LL DO WHAT IT TAKES!"

(JESUS PRAYS THE SECOND TIME)

Then, a second time he went off to pray and his friends fell asleep again. OK, go to sleep, everyone. . . . Now, Jesus asked God to find a way for him to save people without having to die on the cross, but God told him there was no other way. So Jesus said "yes" to God. Then he came back and found everyone sleeping! Some of them were probably snoring . . .

And they sat up . . . and yawned . . . and Jesus said, "I know that you're sleepy, but please stay awake."

And they said, ready? "WE PROMISE YOU, JESUS! WE'LL DO WHAT IT TAKES!"

(JESUS PRAYS THE THIRD TIME)

So Jesus went off a third time and prayed the same thing. Once again he returned and they were sleeping again! But this time he didn't ask them to stay awake. Instead he said, "Look! The man who wants to hurt me is here!"

And they sat up . . . and yawned . . . and stared into the night.

Peter and the rest of the disciples didn't know who Jesus was talking about. Let's all listen and find out what happened!

Below is a monologue, a special way of retelling a story from the perspective of one of the characters in the story. This story is told from Peter's perspective. If you wish, wear a fishing hat or another simple costume piece when you tell the story to show that you are a fisherman. When learning a monologue, follow these seven steps:

1. Read it aloud three times. Don't try to memorize it word for word, just think through the flow of the monologue from one idea to the next.

2. Explain the monologue to yourself in your own words. For example, "This monologue is about . . ."

3. Try to go all the way through the monologue to the end, regardless of whether or not you use the "right" words or remember every detail.

4. Review the script. Look at the sections you forgot; don't worry about specific words. You're trying to make sure you know the sweep of the monologue.

5. Practice it again without the script. Stand up and walk around as you tell it to see what actions feel natural to use.

6. Take a break. Put the script aside, wait a few hours or a day, then pull it out and try it again.

7. Continue reviewing the monologue without the script until you're comfortable with it. Only refer to the script if you get stumped. Remember to go all the way through the script each time rather than starting over if you can't remember a specific word. Relax and have fun!

Hi, my name is Peter and I'm one of Jesus' friends.

Or at least, I used to be. You see, I haven't been a very good friend. Like the night I kept falling asleep when he asked me to stay awake for him.

Jesus said one of us would hurt him. But none of us could figure out what he was talking about.

So then, after he woke us up the third time, we saw a group of soldiers coming toward us through the night. Some of the men were carrying torches; others had swords!

One of the men stepped forward and greeted Jesus. But it wasn't a soldier—it was

Judas! He was the one who wanted to hurt Jesus! Then the guards grabbed Jesus to tie him up!

I jumped at them with a sword, but only managed to cut off this one guy's ear. I've never been very good with a sword—a fishing net, yes—a sword, no . . .

Anyway, Jesus healed that guy and then they took Jesus away and the rest of us . . . well, we ran off into the night.

(Sadly) Later that night, when some people asked me if I was Jesus' friend, I told them I wasn't—three times in a row.

I know it was wrong. I felt so bad about it afterward that I ran off and cried. I wondered if Jesus would ever forgive me for what I'd done.

No, Judas wasn't the only one who had hurt Jesus. We all did.

(If you want to make sure you don't end on a negative note, you could include the following paragraph in Peter's monologue)

Only later did I realize Jesus still loved me! After three days he came back to life and then made sure I knew he wasn't mad at me!

Jesus is the greatest friend any of us could ever have. He died for me and for you and for everyone!

Now, I make sure everyone I meet knows about the power and love of my friend Jesus!

(Take off the fishing hat and set it down. Then say, "Well, Peter sure felt bad after all those things. Especially when he saw them take Jesus away to kill him!")

After the monologue, explain that after Jesus rose from the dead he made sure Peter knew he wasn't mad at him. Jesus forgave and accepted Peter even though Peter had let him down. Jesus loves and accepts us too, even when we let him down. Nothing we could ever do could cause Jesus to stop loving us.

Could Jesus have stopped those men from arresting him? *(Allow them to respond: "YES!")*
Could Jesus have stopped them from hurting him? *("YES!")*
Could Jesus have gotten away if he wanted to? *("YES!")*
Did Jesus forgive those people who hurt him? *("YES!")*
Did Jesus let himself die because he loved them? *("YES!")*
Does Jesus still love us even today? *("YES!")*

Summary

Jesus helped and he healed;
Showed kindness and love;
Told stories of home and his kingdom above.
He talked as if God were his Daddy and Father.
It made quite a stir!
Yes, it caused quite a bother!

For the leaders all hated this talk about "Dad"!
They thought it was wrong,
And they thought it was bad.
So they schemed up a scheme and got people to lie.
And they told Jesus,
    "For breaking our laws you must die!"

They threatened him, hurt him, and just wouldn't quit!
But he never complained.
No, not one little bit.
Even though he was laughed at and spit at and hit!

Then Jesus hung high on a cross and he sighed.
And he said, "It is finished."
And then, Jesus died.[4]

Thank goodness Easter is coming!

Chapter 10

Easter Morning—Jesus Is Alive!

BASED ON: Matthew 27:55–28:10; Mark 15:40–16:11; Luke 24:1-12; and John 20:1-18

BIG IDEA: On Easter morning, Jesus rose from the dead to rescue sinners everywhere.

BACKGROUND: After Jesus rose from the dead, he appeared first to his friend Mary Magdalene (sometimes referred to as Mary of Magdala, since that's the town she was from), a woman out of whom he had cast seven demons.

   At first she was sad when she couldn't find Jesus' body. She thought someone had taken it away, but she soon believed in his resurrection. She spread the news and let others know that Jesus truly had come back to life!

KEY VERSE: "Mary Magdalene went to the disciples with the news: 'I have seen the Lord!'" (John 20:18a).

Children will probably be familiar with this story, but perhaps not familiar with some of the terms or practices of Jewish culture. A "tomb" was where they put dead bodies. The "Sabbath Day" was a special day of rest. Also, they would put spices on dead bodies. So, Mary Magdalene and her friends were heading to do that with Jesus' body on Sunday morning when they found he had risen from the dead.

Also, Jesus had cast seven demons out of Mary Magdalene, but it might be distracting to get into all that, so in the following lesson, I've just said that Jesus helped her feel better.

Read the resurrection accounts in Scripture for yourself before leading today's story. Each of the gospel writers emphasizes different aspects of the story, and it's important to understand the big picture before teaching the story.

Before acting out a story, it's often helpful to tell it to the children first. That way they'll be familiar with the story when they do act it out.[5]

> On the Sunday morning after Jesus had been put in the grave, his friends went to put spices on his body. It was so early in the morning that the sun was just coming up in the sky.
> They were talking about their problem. Jesus was in a cave. And the rock in front of the cave was too big to move! So they were trying to think of a way to move it!
> But when they got there, they saw the rock was moved already! Even though it was a very big rock, it was rolled out of the way!
> Then they saw an angel! The angel told them Jesus was alive again! No one had to move the stone. The angel already had!
> God wanted everyone to know that Jesus was alive!

Read through the following story dramatization several times before leading the activity with the children. Decide if you want to do all of the suggested ideas, or just some of them. Also, as you act out karate-chopping the rock, karate-kicking the rock, or head-butting the rock, be sure to show how painful it is when the rock doesn't break!

> Kids, when the women went to the tomb, they were trying to think of ways to get rid of the big rock that was in the way.

Let's pretend we're trying to move that big rock, OK? Everyone stand up and let's try to lift a giant imaginary rock. Put your hands out and feel the rock. Feel how high it is . . . feel how smooth or rough it is . . . Now, it's gonna be too big to lift, but let's try anyway! Ready? Reach out your hands . . . 1-2-3! *(attempt to lift the rock)* . . . Ugh! The rock is just too BIG!

OK, maybe they thought they could push the rock out of the way! Maybe that'll help! Ready? Put your hands on the imaginary rock. OK. Here we go . . . 1-2-3! . . . Ugh! The rock is just too BIG!

Hmm . . . OK, let's karate chop the rock and see what happens. Ready? Get your karate-chopping hands up and . . . 1-2-3! . . . Ouch! The rock is too HARD and it's just too BIG too!

Let's karate-kick the rock! 1-2-3! . . . Ow, ow, ow!

Let's head-butt the rock! Here we go! 1-2-3! . . . Oooo . . .

Now, pretend you're that angel! Show me how big you are . . . how strong you are . . . OK now, get a little pinky finger ready. You're so strong you'll easily be able to push the rock out of the way . . . OK, 1-2-3 and, push it out of the way! Ping!

Wow! That was easy!

Now, pretend you're that big strong angel and let's all say together, "Jesus is alive!" Let's say it loud because it's good news we want everyone to hear. Ready? "JESUS IS ALIVE!"

Here's another way to retell this story. Teach the children the refrain and explain that each time you'll repeat it twice. Pat your legs to create a beat while you say the refrain. Encourage the children to pat their legs with you. (Be aware that younger children may have a tough time keeping the beat while also singing the words.) Explain that sometimes you'll say the refrain **sadly** . . . and sometimes **excitedly**!

Mary Magdalene was a friend of Jesus. They'd been friends ever since Jesus helped her feel better one day. When he did that, she was so excited she told everyone about it!

(excitedly, with rhythm) Have you heard?
Have you heard?
Have you heard the news about Jesus?
(Repeat)

But now she was sad! Jesus had been arrested! They were going to kill him, even though he hadn't done anything wrong!

(sadly) Have you heard?
Have you heard?
Have you heard the news about Jesus?
(Repeat)

She watched Jesus walk up the hill and saw him get nailed to the cross. Then he died and she was very sad. After he died, she told people the sad news that her friend, the one she had listened to and followed, was dead.

(sadly) Have you heard?
Have you heard?
Have you heard the news about Jesus?
(Repeat)

The next day she rested. Then on Sunday morning, she went to the place where Jesus was buried. She wanted to put spices on his body.

When she got there, she saw some angels! And the angels told her that Jesus wasn't dead, but alive again! And the angels said,

(excitedly) Have you heard?
Have you heard?
Have you heard the news about Jesus?
(Repeat)

"He's not dead! He's alive!"
So Mary ran down the road. She ran back to town. She ran to the home of Peter and John. And when she got there she told them,

(excitedly) Have you heard?
Have you heard?
Have you heard the news about Jesus?
(Repeat)

"He's not in the tomb! Where could he be?"
So Peter and John ran to the tomb. And when they got there, they found it just like she said. Peter didn't know what to think, but John believed that Jesus had come back to life!

(excitedly) Have you heard?
Have you heard?
Have you heard the news about Jesus?
(Repeat)

When Mary got back to the tomb, she saw a man nearby. He asked her why she was so sad.

"They've taken my Lord," she said. "And I don't know where they've put him!"
"Mary, it's me!" said the man by the tomb. "It's me! It's me! It's *ME!*"
Then she knew it was Jesus!

(excitedly) Have you heard?
Have you heard?
Have you heard the news about Jesus?
(Repeat)

And Jesus told her, "I'm not dead! Go and tell my friends I'll see them soon. Tell them I've gone to see my Father and your Father . . . my God and your God! Go and tell them! Go and tell them all!"

So that's just what she did, and it's just what Peter and John did, and it's what you can do too!

(super excitedly) HAVE YOU HEARD?
HAVE YOU HEARD?
HAVE YOU HEARD THE NEWS ABOUT JESUS?
(Repeat)

Summary

For three days it seemed like he'd never arise,
Could his talk and his promises all have been lies?
Could Jesus have lost?
Could the devil have won?
No! The story of Jesus had only begun!
For even before the breaking of dawn,
When they went to the grave they found Jesus was gone!

They were stunned!
They were startled!
And shocked with surprise!
They blinked and they wondered and rubbed at their eyes!
Then an angel appeared and the people soon learned
That Christ wasn't dead, but instead had returned!
Jesus, our Hero, did just what he'd said!
      He died and then came back to life from the dead!
      He did it to rescue us all from our sin,
      God's kingdom was opened,
      So all could come in![6]

Chapter 11

Water into Wine

BASED ON: John 2:1-11

BIG IDEA: Jesus turned six large jars of water into wine at a wedding in Cana. As a result of this, his first miracle, Jesus' disciples believed in him.

BACKGROUND: After being baptized and calling his first disciples, Jesus traveled with them to a wedding in Cana.

When the waiters at the wedding reception ran out of wine, Jesus' mother asked him to do something. Apparently, she knew he was the one to go to for help!

Jesus told her that she needed to let him do things in his own time. Then, he rescued the waiters from the embarrassment of running out of wine by turning six vats of water into wine. News of his power and glory began to spread.

KEY VERSE: "This, the first of his miraculous signs, Jesus performed in Cana in Galilee. He thus revealed his glory, and his disciples put their faith in him" (John 2:11).

Young children might not understand what wine is. You might wish to simply explain that it's a special drink for grown-ups that doesn't taste very good to kids.

Also, be sensitive to the fact that some Christians feel that abstaining from alcohol is an important lifestyle choice for believers. Don't act out drinking wine with the children.

Jewish weddings were important cultural events. They often lasted a week or more and included lots of dancing, drinking, and feasting. The wedding referred to in this story was more like a wedding reception today than a modern marriage ceremony.

For the following story, you may wish to use a real digital camera and take actual pictures of the children, or you might wish to simply pretend to take their pictures. If you use a real camera, you could post the pictures on your church's website and let parents know the link so that they can surf to it at home and have their children retell the story to them with the help of the photos!

Jesus and his friends were at a party to celebrate someone's wedding! At first everyone at the party was happy and dancing. When I count down from three to one, I want you to pretend you're one of those happy, dancing people! But when I yell "Click!" freeze because I'm going to take a (pretend) picture of the wedding dance! I wonder what it will look like? Ready to dance? . . . And then freeze! . . . 3-2-1 Go! . . . And click!

Wow! What a great picture of a wedding dance! *(Pretend to snap a picture of your students.)* **OK, relax and stand normal.**

Now I want to take a picture of the servants. They found out they were going to run out of wine for all the grown-ups! They're very worried! Ready to look worried? . . . 3-2-1 Go! . . . And click! . . . Oh, my! Very good!. OK, relax.

Now Jesus' mother is whispering to Jesus to see if he can help. She doesn't want everyone to know about the problem, so she's trying to be secret and quiet. Ready? . . . 3-2-1 Go! . . . And click! . . . Nice! OK, relax.

Hmm . . . I wonder if Jesus will help? Now Jesus is pointing to six big jars in the corner over there. I think I'll take a picture of Jesus pointing and telling the servants to fill those jars with water. Pretend to be Jesus pointing at the jars! . . . 3-2-1 Go! . . . And click! . . . Good! OK, relax.

Now those servants are carrying lots of water because those jars are really big! They're going to fill the jars with water just like Jesus said. I think I'll take a picture of those servants carrying buckets and buckets of heavy water! Ready to carry your heavy buckets? . . . 3-2-1 Go! . . . And click! . . . OK, relax.

Now they're serving the water to the guests, but it's not water anymore! It's wine! Show me how surprised they are! Ready? . . . 3-2-1 Go! . . . And click! . . . Good!

Oh my goodness! Now the man in charge of the party is having some wine, and he thinks it's the best wine of all! Look how happy he is. Let's see how happy he is. Ready? . . . 3-2-1 Go! . . . And click! . . . Good. You can relax.

Then Jesus' friends believed in him and they decided to follow him with their lives. Pretend that _____ *(choose one of your students)* is Jesus and when I count back from three this time, I want you to start following him and then freeze when I say click. Ready? . . . 3-2-1 Go! Follow Jesus . . . *(wait long enough for them to start following "Jesus")* . . . Click! . . . OK, follow him again. Follow, follow . . . 3-2-1 . . . Click! . . . Follow . . . Click! *(Have some fun with this freezing and following if you wish.)*

Great job, kids!
The end!

Below is a catchy way of telling or reviewing the story. You might wish to use party supplies (plates, cups, party favors) with the children and emphasize how a party wouldn't be as much fun if there wasn't enough to eat or drink. **"Imagine going to a friend's house for a birthday party and in the middle of the party, before everyone gets a piece of cake, they run out of cake! What would happen? Would some people be sad? That's what was about to happen when Jesus was at a party, only it wasn't cake that was getting used up, it was a special drink for grown-ups called wine."**

(With rhythm)
Pretend you're at a party,
A party! A party!
Pretend you're at a party and you're having lots of fun! *(Act like you're at a party)*
(If desired, repeat this refrain after every verse)

Maybe you are eating! *(Let's see some eating!)*
Maybe you are drinking! *(OK, drink some juice!)*
Maybe you are dancing in front of everyone! *(Show me your wildest dance!)*

But the people at the party
Are worried 'cause there's hardly
Wine for all the grown-ups, and soon it will be done! *(Show me how worried they were!)*

So Jesus told the servants
Working at the party
To fill some jars with water and everyone was stunned! *(Show me how surprised they were!)*

The water turned to wine that
Was better than the wine that
They used at the beginning [when the] party had begun! *(Let's give Jesus two thumbs up!)*
Good Job!
(Repeat the entire chant)

Summary

The party had started, the wine had been poured,
All the people were eating and no one was bored!
The families were happy and beaming with pride,
At the handsome young groom and his beautiful bride.

The servants piled food on everyone's plate,
But then came some news that wasn't so great.
The wine they were drinking was getting used up!
And soon they would drink up the very last cup!

Now Mary knew Jesus was perfect and good,
So she asked him to help and she knew that he would.
But he told her, "Be patient; the time isn't right.
Just trust that I'll know when to help them tonight."

Then he looked at the worry on the servants' faces,
And he showed them all some really big vases.
And then without drawing too much attention to him,
He whispered, "Fill them up. Fill them up to the brim.
     Fill the vases with water 'til they look pretty bursty,
     Then serve what's inside to the guests who are thirsty."

So they did as he said, and then when they were done,
They had plenty of wine to serve everyone!
For the water inside of the cups that they filled,
Had all turned to wine and the people were thrilled!
     And this wine was quite tasty and delicious and fine
     And it tasted so yummy and fresh from the vine!

"It's the best wine of all!" said a guy who was there.
"No, nothing I've had up 'til now can compare!"
And that's when the friends of Jesus believed—
When they sipped from the miracle wine they received.

Chapter 12

Nets Full of Fish

BASED ON: Luke 5:1-11

BIG IDEA: When we discover the true identity of Jesus, our lives are changed forever.

BACKGROUND: Even though the first disciples (Peter, Andrew, James, and John) had started to follow Jesus, they hadn't truly recognized who he really was. One day, after a miraculous catch of fish, they left their nets behind and followed Jesus for good. When we recognize the true identity of Christ, our lives are changed forever as well.

KEY VERSE: "Then Jesus said to Simon, 'Don't be afraid; from now on you will catch men.' So they pulled their boats up on shore, left everything and followed him" (Luke 5:10, 11).

John also records a miraculous catch of fish (see John 21). Some Bible scholars believe that John and Luke are referring to the same account, but others see enough differences to trust that these are two distinctly different stories—one that happened at the beginning of Jesus' ministry on earth (see Luke's story), and one that happened at the very end (see John's account).

When telling the following sound effects story, remember to practice it a couple of times before class to learn the rhythm of the sound effects. Remind the children that you'll be saying each refrain one time by yourself, and then they'll join along saying it two additional times. **"Remember, we'll only say each thing three times so we can all hear the rest of the story!"**

Feel free to use appropriate voice inflection as you tell the story. For example, during the exciting parts you can make your voice sound excited, or during happy parts sound happy and relieved. Also, if desired you may wish to do the suggested actions as you say each refrain.

STORY:	REFRAINS:	SUGGESTED ACTIONS:
One day, Jesus' friends went out fishing.	Row! Row! Row-y row! Row! Row! Row-y row! Row! Row! Row-y row!	Row your boats!
It was nighttime when they went.	Yawn. Yawn. Yawny yawn! Yawn. Yawn. Yawny yawn! Yawn. Yawn. Yawny yawn!	Yawn.
Back then, they'd go fishing by tossing nets out into the water.	Splash. Splash. Splashy splash. Splash. Splash. Splashy splash. Splash. Splash. Splashy splash.	Toss your nets!
All night, they tossed their nets out and then dragged them back in again.	Drag. Drag. Draggy drag. Drag. Drag. Draggy drag. Drag. Drag. Draggy drag.	Pull your nets in!
But each time the nets were empty!	Bum. Bum. Bummer bum. Bum. Bum. Bummer bum. Bum. Bum. Bummer bum.	Snap your finger. You're disappointed.
Finally, they rowed back to shore and started cleaning their nets.	Scrub. Scrub. Scrub-a-dub! Scrub. Scrub. Scrub-a-dub! Scrub. Scrub. Scrub-a-dub!	Scrub your nets.

Meanwhile, Jesus was preaching to the people,	Talk. Talk. Talky talk. Talk. Talk. Talky talk. Talk. Talk. Talky talk.	Pretend to preach.
And there were so many people on the beach, he was getting crowded into the water!	Shove! Shove! Shove-y shove! Shove! Shove! Shove-y shove! Shove! Shove! Shove-y shove!	Shove an imaginary person next to you.
So, he climbed onto Peter's boat,	Climb. Climb. Climb aboard. Climb. Climb. Climb aboard. Climb. Climb. Climb aboard.	Climb up!
He finished preaching, and then he excused the people.	Bye. Bye. Bye goodbye! Bye. Bye. Bye goodbye! Bye. Bye. Bye goodbye!	Wave goodbye.
Then, he asked if he could go fishing with the guys, and they said yes.	OK. Kay. Kay OK. OK. Kay. Kay OK. OK. Kay. Kay OK.	Nod. Two thumbs up.
Then, he told them to toss the nets out and when they did, the nets immediately filled with fish!	Whoa. Whoa. Whoa-y whoa! Whoa. Whoa. Whoa-y whoa! Whoa. Whoa. Whoa-y whoa!	Look surprised.
The nets were so full, they started to tear apart!	Rip! Rip! Rippy rip! Rip! Rip! Rippy rip! Rip! Rip! Rippy rip!	Rip the nets.
Then, the boats started to sink!	Blub. Blub. Blubby blub. Blub. Blub. Blubby blub. Blub. Blub. Blubby blub.	Grab your nose with one hand, wave with the other.
Peter realized Jesus was from God, and he was scared of him!	Yikes! Yikes! Yike-y yikes! Yikes! Yikes! Yike-y yikes! Yikes! Yikes! Yike-y yikes!	Be scared!
They made it back to the shore.	Hip! Hip! Hip hooray! Hip! Hip! Hip hooray! Hip! Hip! Hip hooray!	Smiles! Lots of cheering!
And Jesus invited the men to be his followers and they left to be with Jesus!	Go, go, go with God! Go, go, go with God! Go, go, go with God!	Walk in place.
The end!		

Explain that Jesus invited the men to fish for people. **"Did he really mean people were sinking in the water? . . . Did he really mean that people eat worms? . . . No! He meant they needed to be drawn to God just like fishermen pull fish into the boat!"**

After telling the story with sound effects, invite the children to act out the story by joining you in the following story dramatization.

OK everyone, let's pretend we are those fishermen! OK, push your boat off from shore . . . And grab your oars and let's row our boat out to the sea. Are there big waves? (rock back and forth) **. . . Whoa! These waves are huge! Don't let the boat tip over! . . .**

Let's row faster . . . And faster . . . And faster! . . . And faster! Good! Now slower rowing . . . Be a slower rower . . . An even slower rower . . .

Now, let's drop the nets into the water. Splash! . . . OK then, we wait for some fish to swim into our nets . . . (yawn) **. . . That should be long enough.**

Pull the nets back in . . . Wow, it's easy to pull them in today! Well, look! There's no fish there! Bummer! Everyone say, "Bummer!" . . . "BUMMER!"

Were they happy or sad when they saw they hadn't caught any fish? . . . Let's see those sad faces . . .

All right, let's row back to shore. . . . Faster rower . . . Slower rower . . . Faster rower . . . Slower rower . . . Faster . . . Slower . . .

Now, we're tired because we've been fishing all night long! *(yawn)* . . . Hmm, I guess before we can go to sleep we need to put the nets away . . . Gather up your nets . . . But who's this? It's Jesus! He wants to get on our boat so he can talk to the people! OK, drop the nets on the deck of the boat . . . and shove 'em to the side to make room for Jesus! . . .

Everyone say, "Come on aboard, Jesus!". . . "COME ON ABOARD, JESUS!"

Great! Let's push the boat away from shore again . . . Wait for Jesus to finish, and now wave goodbye to the people . . .

Now Jesus is asking us to go fishing! OK, here we go again . . . Faster rower . . . Slower rower . . . Faster rower . . . Slower rower . . . Faster . . . Slower . . .

Now he wants us to drop the nets over the side of the boat! Let's see what happens when we do. Drop your nets . . . Pull them back in . . . Oh, no! It's too hard to pull in the nets! They're full of fish! Pull harder . . . Harder . . . Harder . . . Oh, my! I can barely pull in my nets at all! Look at all the fish!

The boat is tipping over—everyone tip to the side! . . . Don't let it tip over! Use your oars! Let's row to shore . . . *(Grunt)* . . . It's hard rowing with all these fish in the nets! . . . Hurry! We have to row to shore before we sink! . . . *(Lots of grunting and rowing.)*

Are you surprised all these fish are in the nets? Show me how surprised you are! . . . Wow! You're really surprised! OK, let's climb out of the boat . . .

OK everyone, let's follow Jesus! *(point to one of the students)* _____ will pretend to be Jesus! Everyone follow him (her)! Let's go. I wonder where he's going to walk or what he's going to do? *(play a short game of Follow the Leader!)*

The end.

After playing a game of Follow the Leader, review the story with the children and remind them that when Jesus' friends saw his power, they realized he was someone very special, someone who was perfect in every way! They left everything to follow him.

Jesus invited them to come with him to cast out nets of love and draw people in, closer to God! **"They left their fishing nets and boats and even those fish behind and followed Jesus. Sometimes we need to leave things behind when we follow Jesus—things like arguing and fighting and biting and talking back to our parents. God loves us so much he's inviting us to share his love with people and draw them closer to God just like those fishermen did long ago!"**

Finally, you can end the lesson by teaching or singing the following song to the tune of "Row, Row, Row Your Boat."

Row, row, row your boat,
Gently in the lake!
See if we can catch a fish
To roast or boil or bake!
(Repeat)

Pull, pull, pull your nets.
Back up toward the boat!
Now the nets are full of fish,
It's tough for us to float!
(Repeat)

Leave, leave, leave the boat
With all those flopping fish!
Follow Jesus where he leads,
And do his every wish.
(Repeat)

Summary

The night was long and the fishing was bad.
And the friends of Jesus were not very glad.
For despite what they hoped
　　　　And despite what they wished,
Not one of four brothers had brought in a fish!

Now Jesus was preaching to a crowd by the shore,
But they crowded around more than ever before,
So he stepped on the boat and then finished his sermon.
And when he was done, he asked all those fishermen
　　　　"Do you want to go fishing? The day is just right!"
But Peter said, "Lord we've been fishing all night
　　　　And we haven't had even one nibble or bite!"

But they pushed out and dropped all their nets in the lake,
As the nets filled with fish and they started to break!
　　　　(And I think that their boat began to shiver and shake!)
Peter was shocked at what Jesus could do
　　　　"Go away!" he said, "I'm not holy like you!"
But Jesus said, "Peter, follow me and you'll see
How amazing fishing for people can be!"

So they rowed back to land and they followed the Lord.
And they left all their nets and their boats on the shore.
　　　　And they gave Jesus more of their faith than before.

Chapter 13

Bringing Down the House!

BASED ON: Mark 2:1-12 (see also Matthew 9:1-8; Luke 5:17-26)

BIG IDEA: When Jesus saw the faith of a disabled man's friends, he not only healed the man, but forgave his sins.

BACKGROUD: The religious teachers were on the lookout to catch Jesus doing something wrong so that they could get rid of him. In this wonderful little story, Jesus is preaching in a house packed with people when four friends come up, carrying their disabled friend. Undaunted by the crowd, they climb up on the roof, dig a hole, and lower him down in front of Jesus!

Jesus affirms the faith of the men who refused to let something get in the way of bringing their friend to Jesus. Then Jesus not only healed the man's body, but also forgave his sins.

KEY VERSE: "He said to the paralytic, 'I tell you, get up, take your mat and go home.' He got up, took his mat and walked out in full view of them all. This amazed everyone and they praised God, saying, 'We have never seen anything like this!'" (Mark 2:10-12).

This is a rather strange story when you think about it. Kids may ask some obvious questions like, "Who fixed the hole?" "Were the people who owned the house mad about the hole?" or, "Why didn't the men just wait until Jesus was finished talking?" We don't know the answers to these questions. Instead, remind the children about what we *do* know. This story shows us the attitudes different groups of people had toward Jesus: the regular people loved to hear him and many trusted that he could do miracles; the religious leaders did not believe in him and wanted to catch him making a mistake.

This would be a fun story to act out with a sleeping bag or sleeping mat. Have one child lie on it and then take turns carrying her around the room!

As you tell the following story, tell the children they will be saying, "Cool!" and then "Bummer!" Encourage them to put two thumbs up or two thumbs down, and also to show by their facial expression if it's good (cool) or bad (bummer).

STORY:	REFRAINS:
Jesus was teaching and helping the people.	Cool!
But there were so many people, they were packed into a house and barely had room to move!	Bummer.
Four friends came to see Jesus.	Cool!
They brought a fifth man along, but he couldn't walk.	Bummer.
So, they were carrying him on a mat!	Cool!
But they couldn't fit into the house to see Jesus!	Bummer.
So they climbed on the roof!	Cool!
Carrying their friend!	Bummer.
Then, they dug a hole right in the middle of the roof!	Cool!
And almost fell in!	Bummer.
Then, they lowered their friend down into the house. He was still lying on his mat!	Cool!
He almost landed on Jesus!	Bummer.
But he didn't!	Cool!
But Jesus had to stop teaching the people.	Bummer.
But Jesus said, "Friend, your sins are forgiven!"	Cool!

But some men didn't like it when Jesus said that!	Bummer.
Because they knew that only God can forgive our sins.	Cool!
But they didn't think Jesus was God!	Bummer.
So Jesus healed the guy to show them all that he could both forgive sins and heal people!	Cool!
But those guys were still mad at him!	Bummer.
But everyone else was really happy and impressed with Jesus!	Cool!
Even though someone had to fix up that hole in the roof—	Bummer.
It was worth it because a man had been healed and had his sins forgiven!	Cool!
The end.	Bummer.
Um, we have to stop now. I'm not going to say anything else.	Cool!
We're done!	Bummer.
I'm leaving.	Cool!

For the following story, encourage the children to repeat the sayings with you after you say them the first time. Add your own ideas if you like!

Jesus was in a house and it was packed with people! *(owie, owie, don't step on my toe!)* He was telling them all about God! *(cool, very cool, God is very, very cool)*.

Now, four men were outside the house and couldn't get in because it was so packed with all those people *(owie, owie, don't step on my toe!)*. They were carrying a guy on a mat who wasn't able to walk *(boy am I thankful for all my friends!)*.

So, when they saw they couldn't get in—because of all those people *(owie, owie, don't step on my toe!)*, they carried the guy on the mat *(boy am I thankful for all my friends!)* up onto the roof! *(don't look down! it's a long way down!)*.

Then, they dug a hole in the roof *(careful, now! don't fall in!)*.

And lowered the man on the mat *(boy am I thankful for all my friends!)* down in front of Jesus, who was telling the people about God *(cool, very cool, God is very, very cool)*.

Jesus forgave that man's sins *(cool, very cool, God is very, very cool)* and even healed him so that he could pick up his mat and walk out the door, past that crowd of people! *(owie, owie, don't step on my toe!)*.

He was thankful to Jesus *(cool, very cool, God is very, very cool)* for being healed and forgiven.

And thankful to his friends for all their help! *(boy am I thankful for all my friends!)*.

Yes, Jesus is powerful enough to help heal both our bodies and our hearts *(cool, very cool, God is very, very cool)*.

The end!

Summary

The house was so full. The house was so crowded.
People came to see Jesus and crowded about him.
While a small group of friends who were outside the door,
Had a buddy who was hurt and couldn't walk anymore.

They knew Christ could heal him and help him to walk.
But they couldn't get into the house where he taught.
Yet they trusted in Jesus—no, they didn't need proof.
So they took their friend up on the top of the roof!

Then they dug out a hole and they lowered him down,
On ropes so their friend wouldn't smack on the ground!
And when Jesus saw their faith he was glad so he said,
   "I forgive all the sins of the man on this bed!"

Yet when the crowd heard that, they started to talk!
But then Jesus healed him and told him to walk!
For healing his body wasn't all he could do
Jesus also forgave all his wrongdoings, too!

Chapter 14

The Man Who Couldn't Walk

BASED ON: John 5:1-15

BIG IDEA: Jesus healed a man who had been lame for 38 years, and no one seemed to be excited by it.

BACKGROUND: When Jesus entered Jerusalem, he walked past a pool with special healing properties. There, he met a man who had been paralyzed for 38 years. Jesus healed him.

Perhaps the most remarkable thing about this story is the lack of joy and celebration after the miracle. We have no record of the man thanking Jesus, and the Pharisees never even show a shred of compassion as they whine about the healed man carrying his sleeping mat away from the pool!

In this story, Jesus' love and compassion shine in sharp contrast to the cold legalism of the Pharisees.

KEY VERSE: "Jesus said to him, 'Get up! Pick up your mat and walk.' At once the man was cured; he picked up his mat and walked" (John 5:8, 9).

One thing we can learn from this story is to be more thankful for the good things Jesus does for us. A good way to teach a value or virtue like "thankfulness" is to show an example of someone who is not thankful, such as the man in this story. You may even wish to tell a story from your life of a time when you received something good from God, but instead of being thankful, you complained (either to God or to other people) about the situation.

This would be a fun story to retell by using props! Gather together the following props before class and then practice telling the story a few times so you won't have to read it from the book, but will be able to retell it in your own words while you manipulate the props.

What you'll need:
- three Barbie dolls, action figures, or dolls (one of them will represent Jesus)
- bowl of water
- small towel or blanket (to serve as the man's sleeping mat)

Decide which of the dolls will represent the man whom Jesus healed (he'll be referred to in the script as "Bob"), which one will be Jesus, and which will represent all the other people healed at the pool (during the script this person will be referred to as the "other guy").

WHAT TO SAY:	SUGGESTED ACTION:
Long ago there was a special pool in Jerusalem . . .	Hold up the bowl of water, show it to the children, and then set it down in view of the students.
People who were sick would gather around it . . .	Hold up the other guy near the pool.
And sometimes, on special days, an angel would go into the pool and swirl the water around . . .	Stir the water with your finger.
I guess I'll be the angel today . . .	Stir it some more.
And when the water was swirled, the first person into the pool	Dip the other guy into the water. Splash around a little if you want.
Would be healed!	Make him dance around! (Spraying water on your children if you wish!)
Well, there was one guy who'd been sitting there for 38 years, and this man couldn't walk.	Make Bob sit down near the pool on the washcloth.

And whenever the angel would swirl the water	Stir the water with your finger.
Someone else would rush into the water in front of the man.	Dip the other guy into the water again.
And be healed!	Dance him around again.
So the guy who couldn't walk was angry.	Shake Bob around angrily.
Well, one day Jesus came walking along and asked the guy if he wanted to be healed.	Make Jesus approach Bob.
The man said, "Whenever the angel swirls the water,	Stir the water again.
someone else gets in there in front of me!"	Dip the other guy into the water again.
And gets healed!	Dance the other guy around again.
Then, Jesus told him to stand up, pick up his sleeping mat, and go home. And he did!	Make Jesus walk away in one direction and Bob in another carrying the washcloth.
Well, some of the leaders asked the guy why he was carrying his sleeping mat on the day of rest. And he said, "The guy who healed me told me to!" So he set down the mat and walked away.	Make Bob shake his head and then have him set down his washcloth and then leave.
Later, Jesus met up with the man and warned him to turn to God.	Bring Bob and Jesus together.
But the man just walked away without ever saying, "Thank you!" to Jesus.	Make Bob walk away.
And then Jesus went off to help more people.	Make Jesus walk away.
So when God helps you out, Remember to say, "I thank you dear Jesus! I thank you today!" Let's say that together: "I THANK YOU DEAR JESUS! I THANK YOU TODAY!" The end.	

Another way to tell this story would be to invite the children to act out the story with you. Get a blue blanket to represent the pool. (Or, put tape on the floor to represent where the pool is.)

Kids, let's pretend that we were there when Jesus healed that man! I need some kids to be the water . . . And some kids to be the people who need to be healed . . . and one person to be the angel (you could use more than one child for the angel, if you wish).

OK, the water starts in here, in the pool . . .

And the angel starts over there, on the other side of the room . . .

Now, all you hurt people have to decide what's wrong with you. Maybe you have a broken arm . . . or you can't walk . . . or you're blind . . . or maybe your big toe hurts! OK, let's hear all those hurt people groan . . .

Now, let's have the angel fly over here . . . Flap your angel wings! . . . And go into the pool, and swirl the water around! OK water, if the angel taps you, spin around in circles! . . .

OK, who's first to get healed? . . . All right angel, fly away . . . And now step into the swirling water. Remember, you're hurting when you step in . . . but then you are healed! . . . and you step out all happy and smiley!

But one guy couldn't get to the pool, so Jesus helped him and healed him. He picked up his mat and walked away!

Repeat as desired until each child has had a chance to be "healed" or has had a chance to be the water or the angel!

Explain to the children that Jesus can heal someone just by talking to them. Jesus is just as powerful today as he used to be. He may not always choose to heal us when we come to him, but if he doesn't give us what we ask for he will give us something even better.

Summary

Lots of people needed healing; lots of people were waiting
By the pool for the angel who came there creating
A swirl in the water and a twirling around
And the first person in would get healed,
        And not drowned!

But one man couldn't walk so he couldn't get in.
When the angel arrived to make the healing begin.
Then when Jesus walked up to the place where he sat
He told him, "Stand up and pick up your mat!"

And without saying thanks, the man went away
He stood up and walked off from Jesus that day!
About then, some leaders saw him carrying that mat
And they weren't very happy at all about that.

(For they thought that since this was their day of rest
Carrying mats around town wasn't really the best.)
But he said, "Someone made me, so I'm not to blame!
It's the same guy who healed me, but I don't know his name."

Later on Jesus told him, "Follow God and stop sinning
Or you'll end up worse off than at the beginning!"
So the man went back to the leaders and said,
"It's Jesus who told me to pick up my bed."

Chapter 15

Jesus Calms the Big Storm

BASED ON: Matthew 8:23-27; Mark 4:35-41; and Luke 8:22-25

BIG IDEA: Jesus revealed his power by commanding the wind and the waves to be still—to the utter amazement of his disciples.

BACKGROUND: One evening, Jesus and his followers sailed out across the lake in a number of boats. During the night, a squall blew in, threatening to sink all the ships. His followers feared for their lives, but then, when he calmed the storm, they were amazed and afraid of him.

   This story shows us a good example of both the divine and the human natures of Christ. His humanity is revealed by his sleeping on the boat (God doesn't sleep). His divinity is revealed by his power over the natural elements (humans can't tell storms what to do). Jesus couldn't be only a God or only a man; in a wonderfully mysterious way, he is totally both!

KEY VERSE: "He got up and rebuked the wind and the raging waters; the storm subsided, and all was calm. 'Where is your faith?' he asked his disciples. In fear and amazement they asked one another, 'Who is this? He commands even the winds and the water, and they obey him'" (Luke 8:24, 25).

The disciples were frightened when they saw Jesus' power over the wind and the waves, but you may not want to emphasize that fear too much when you tell the story. Yes, Jesus is mighty and powerful, but he is also loving and accepting. We don't need to tremble in fear at God's power, but rather worship him because of it.

This is a fun story to tell and a fun one to act out. In Appendix C you'll find a number of creative ideas for retelling this story with sounds, objects, actions, and repetition. Here are two additional ways to tell this story.

> **Dribble drip,**
> **Dribble drip,**
> **Dribble drip, drop.**
> **A big storm was coming and just wouldn't stop!**
> **Everyone pretend that you're a raindrop! Let's see you fall to the ground! . . . Float up again . . . and fall . . . float . . . and fall . . . float . . . and fall . . .**
> **Are you a big round raindrop or a small, little, tiny one? . . . All right all you raindrops, fall to the deck of the ship and spread out into a puddle . . .**
>
> **Whoosh and blow!**
> **Whoosh and blow!**
> **Whoosh and blow, wind**
> **Was pushing the boat further out and not in!**
> **OK everyone, now you're the wind! . . . Blow around the room a little bit! Jesus' friends were on a boat and a great big wind was blowing! Show me how big you are! . . . Are you a fast wind? . . . Are you a strong wind? . . . Are you a mean wind? . . .**
> **OK wind, blow into the sail and be still for a moment.**
>
> **Crash and curl!**
> **Crash and curl!**
> **Crash and curl, splash!**

Big waves were splashing while lightning bolts flashed!
Wave your arms out like big waves on the ocean! . . . And rock back and forth . . . Back and forth . . . You're great big waves splashing all over the ocean! And keep flowing back and forth, but you're not going to be waves for long!

Tip and flip,
Tip and flip,
Tip and flip, No!
The boat is about to go sinking below!
Now pretend that you're one of Jesus' friends! You're trying to make sure the boat doesn't tip over! . . . Grab your oars and push them against the strong waves! . . . Or maybe pull down the sail so it doesn't rip! . . . Pull it down! Pull it down! Pull it down!
Remember, you're tipping back and forth as those waves push against the boat!
But now, we're going to change into someone else. Ready?

Snore and sleep,
Snore and sleep,
Snore and sleep, nap!
Jesus is snoozing while thunderclouds clap!
OK kids, let's all lie down . . . It's been a long day and you're very tired . . . All you want to do is go to sleep . . .
I wonder if anyone in here snores? . . . Oh my, we have some loud snorers! . . . Then the disciples said,

"Wake up, please!
Wake up, please!
Wake up, please, Lord!
We're all gonna drown in this terrible storm!"

Wanna say that with me?
"WAKE UP, PLEASE!
WAKE UP, PLEASE!
WAKE UP, PLEASE, LORD!
WE'RE ALL GONNA DROWN IN THIS TERRIBLE STORM!"

OK kids, pretend that you are Jesus and your friends just woke you up . . . They're scared the boat is going to sink! But you're not scared! Stand up . . . And ready? Hold up your hand like Jesus might have done! Let's tell the storm to be quiet!

"Calm down now!
Calm down now!
Be calm and be still!
Don't try to tip us or make the boat spill!"

Let's all say Jesus' part together, OK?
"CALM DOWN NOW!
CALM DOWN NOW!
BE CALM AND BE STILL!
DON'T TRY TO TIP US OR MAKE THE BOAT SPILL!"

Now, do I have the power to tell a big storm what to do? . . . No! Of course not! Do you? . . . No! But does Jesus? . . . Yes, he does!

When the waves and the wind heard Jesus tell them to be quiet, they did! And Jesus' friends all knew Jesus was from Heaven because no one from earth can tell storms what to do!

The end.

Consider having one other adult (or teen volunteer) up front to help you with the following story. That person will be Jesus while you act as the storyteller!

WHAT TO SAY:	WHAT TO DO:
Boys and girls, Jesus went out on the boat . . .	Jesus enters, smiling, and walks to center stage.
The disciples all got into the boat too, but Jesus just lay down and went to sleep . . .	Jesus lies down, grabs a teddy bear, snuggles up and goes to sleep.
Soon a storm blew in! The disciples were all scared—but Jesus was still fast asleep.	Snore away, Jesus!
He didn't wake up when the storm blew in!	Turn on a fan and aim it at Jesus.
He didn't wake up when the lightning flashed!	Flicker the lights in your room on and off.
He didn't wake up when the raindrops fell!	Spray some water at Jesus with a squirt gun or a spray bottle.
He didn't wake up when the thunder boomed!	Get close to Jesus' ear and yell, "Boom! Boom! Boom! Boom!"
He didn't even wake up when the boat rocked back and forth!	Rock Jesus back and forth.
He must have been really tired! So the disciples had to wake Jesus up. Maybe they shook him.	Shake Jesus.
Or maybe they yelled in his ear.	Yell in Jesus' ear, "Wake up! We're all gonna die over here!"
Finally, Jesus woke up.	Jesus yawns, stretches his arms.
The disciples were freaking out. "We're all gonna die!" But Jesus wasn't worried in the least.	Jesus shakes his head "no" and sighs.
Then Jesus told the wind and the waves to go to sleep, and they did.	Jesus says something like, "Chill with the storm, already, OK?" Or he could say, "Quiet down wind, and waves settle down! We're not gonna sink and we're not gonna drown!"
His friends were amazed at him, and Jesus said, "Why did you ever doubt?"	Jesus says, "Why did you ever doubt?"
And they were like, "What kind of guy is this who even tells the wind and the waves what to do?"	Jesus says, "I'm Jesus. That says it all."
The end!	Bow and take a seat.

You may wish to think of other creative ways to have the students help you recreate the storm, the wind, and the waves. Consider handing them colored crepe paper to wave above their heads, fans to flutter in the air, or blue blankets to ripple as the waves come rolling in.

Summary

The disciples and Jesus
Got into a boat
And they headed out onto the lake.
But soon the waves grew,
And a great big wind blew,
And they thought that their boat would soon break!

Now Jesus was tired,
And lay fast asleep
On the boat as his friends all got scared.
Then they gave him a shake,
To shake him awake,
"We're all gonna die!" they declared.

So he spoke to the wind
And he spoke to the waves
And he told them to please quiet down.
Then he told the disciples
"If you'd only believe
Then you'd know that we're not gonna drown!"

And when they all saw
How he spoke to the wind
And heard him tell waves what to do.
His friends were afraid.
At the strength he displayed.
And they knew that his power was true.

Chapter 16

The Really Big Picnic

BASED ON: Matthew 14:13-21; Mark 6:30-44; Luke 9:10-17; and John 6:1-15

BIG IDEA: Jesus miraculously fed a crowd of thousands, and then used the miracle to encourage the people to satisfy their spiritual longings by "feeding on" him.

BACKGROUND: After John the Baptist was killed in prison, his followers buried his body and then reported the news to Jesus. When he heard about it, Jesus left with his disciples to find a quiet place to pray and rest. He needed a chance to mourn the passing of his dear friend and relative.

But the people heard where he was going, and by the time his boat reached the beach, there was already a large crowd (five thousand men plus women and children) waiting for them.

Jesus had compassion on them. He taught, healed, and then fed them. Later, he was able to use this miracle as an object lesson to discuss the true nature of his ministry. Yet, only after his resurrection did his followers realize the true meaning and importance of his words.

KEY VERSE: "Then Jesus declared, 'I am the bread of life. He who comes to me will never go hungry, and he who believes in me will never be thirsty'" (John 6:35).

When you're researching this story to tell it to the children, be sure to read the broader context of the verses and not just the account of the feeding of the five thousand families. It's important to know that even after all that he'd done, the people still demanded a sign and followed Jesus to get body food, not soul food.

While it's true that Jesus has the power to heal our physical diseases and care for our physical needs, he came with an even greater purpose in mind—to fulfill our spiritual hungers. Explain to the children that Jesus came to feed hungry hearts, not just hungry tummies.

This is a rather popular story for children's Bible lessons, probably because there is a child in it. We don't really know what the boy's motivation was, or even if he really wanted to share his food. However, we do know that Jesus was able to use the boy's food to bless a whole group of people.

The success of the following story rests on how playfully you present it. Each time you ask the children a question and they yell out, "Fish and Bread!" get more and more frustrated that they already know the answers. The children will love how they seem to know something you don't, and may get so excited that you will have trouble calming them down!

One day Jesus was teaching, and lots of people were there—five thousand men plus lots of women and children! And everyone was hungry, so Jesus sent out a couple of his friends to find some food. And they found a little boy who had five loaves of *something* and two *somethings that swim in the water* to eat.

Now you'll never guess in a million, billion years what they had *five loaves of*—(allow *them to respond, and then act really surprised that they knew the answer*) **. . . How did you know that? How did you know it was BREAD?**

Well, you'll never guess what they had two of that *swim in the water*—(allow them to *respond; act even more surprised*) **. . . How did you know that? How did you know it was FISH?**

Is someone telling you the answers? . . . You're telling me they found a boy with *fish and bread?* . . .

Well, you're right.

So then, Jesus thanked God for the food and then he handed out *something* to the people. You'll never guess what he gave them to eat *(allow them to respond. You're amazed they keep getting it right)* . . . How did you know it was *fish and bread?* Who told you it was *fish and bread?*

All right. All right. Well, everyone started to break off a little bit of something and eat it—*(by now the children will probably be interrupting you to say "Fish and bread!" That's OK! Play off what they say; get more and more exasperated each time).*

And then they handed the stuff to the other people. But you'll never ever guess what they handed them—*(you get the routine).* HOW DID YOU KNOW IT WAS FISH AND BREAD?

And those people broke off some and ate some—you'll never guess what they ate—

And pretty soon everyone there had eaten all that they wanted of that—

And when they were done, Jesus had his friends pick up all the leftover—

And there were twelve baskets full of—!

Yes, Jesus had fed a crowd of more than five thousand people with just a handful of—

And at the end there was even more—

Than at the beginning!

The end!

You could also present this story as a monologue, told from the perspective of the boy's mother. Use a scarf or other simple costume piece to help create the character you are portraying.

My son always gets so hungry! So I packed him a lunch—a couple of fish sandwiches. Yummy. He loooovvvveeees fish sandwiches!

We went to hear Jesus teach. There were thousands and thousands of people there that day!

So then, what happens? These two guys come up and ask my son if he's got any food and he says, "Yeah, my mom packed a couple of fish sandwiches. Yummy! I loooovvvveeee fish sandwiches!"

And they were like, "Well, then. Come with us. Jesus wants to see you."

Jesus wanted to see my son! Wow, how cool is that?

And then Jesus asks my son for his lunch and I figure, huh, Jesus must be hungry, right? But then he says a prayer and he breaks the bread in half and the fish in half and he hands the food to one of his friends. Philip, I think his name was. And Philip was like, "Oh goody-goody-gumdrops! Fish sandwiches. Yummy! I loooovvvveeee fish sandwiches!"

And Jesus was like, "Take some and pass it along. Share with everyone!"

And that's what the people did! They took some and ate some and passed some around. And they were like, "Oh, goody-goody-gumdrops! Fish sandwiches. Yummy! We loooovvvveeee fish sandwiches!"

So we all had supper then, right? All of us! And at the end they gathered up twelve baskets full of leftovers of fish sandwiches. Yummy! I loooovvvveeee fish sandwiches!

I wish I knew how to do that trick, especially when I'm trying to feed my husband. Oy!

Well, anyway. I was so proud of my son, sharing his food like that! And I was so amazed at Jesus who did such a wonderful miracle and fed all those people with only a couple of fish sandwiches. Yummy! I loooovvvveeee fish sandwiches!

Summary

The crowds that came crowding around him that day
Listened carefully to all that the Lord had to say.
And then when his teaching was done for the day
The disciples tried to send all the people away.

But Jesus said, "No, for they'd like a small treat;
So why don't you give them all something to eat?"
Well, none of the disciples thought that was too funny
'Cause they didn't have food and they didn't have money.
 "There're thousands of people all hungry!" they said.
 "And we haven't the bread for these folks to be fed!"

Then Andrew and Philip found a boy who had brought
Five loaves of bread and two fish that he'd caught.
"That's plenty," said Jesus. Then he said a short prayer
And he handed the food to the folks who were there.

They broke it and passed it and broke it some more,
And each time they broke it, there was more than before!
Until everyone sitting out there on the ground
Had eaten their fill and gobbled it down!

Then Jesus had 'em gather the food that was spilled,
And when they were done, twelve baskets were filled!
In the end all those people were full and were grinning,
And there was more food then than at the beginning!

Chapter 17

Walking on the Water

BASED ON: Matthew 14:22-33

BIG IDEA: Jesus walked on the water and displayed his power to the disciples. As a result, they worshiped him.

BACKGROUND: After Jesus had finished feeding the five thousand people, he excused them and then sent his disciples out on a boat toward the other side of the lake.

It's significant to note that Jesus made the disciples get into the boat (see Matthew 14:22). He knew he was going to walk across the water and this instance gave them another display of his power and another chance to grow in their faith.

KEY VERSE: "Then Peter got down out of the boat, walked on the water and came toward Jesus. But when he saw the wind, he was afraid and, beginning to sink, cried out, 'Lord, save me!' Immediately Jesus reached out his hand and caught him. 'You of little faith,' he said, 'why did you doubt?'" (Matthew 14:29, 31).

Stories are typically about a transformation of a person or a situation. This story is a good example. When the storm first blows in, the disciples are terrified. When they see Jesus they are uncertain, and when he gets into the boat they bow to worship him as their Lord. By the end of the story, the storm (their outer struggle) is calmed, and their terror (their inner struggle) is transformed into worship!

While this is certainly a story about all of the disciples, the main character is Peter who stepped out of the boat, struggled with doubting Jesus, and was then rescued by the Lord.

For the following story, teach the children to echo the refrain after you say each line. When good things happen in the story, you'll say, "Huh, huh, yeah!" and when bad things happen you'll say, "Huh, huh, bad!" Here is the refrain:

(with rhythm)
>   **He was walkin' on the water . . .** *(Children repeat)*
>   *(Say it louder and more exaggerated)* **I said walkin' on the water! . . .** *(Children repeat, getting wilder and louder)*
>   *(Real loud, really exaggerated)* **WALKIN' ON THE WATER!** *(Children repeat, getting really wild and loud)*
>   **Huh, huh, yeah! . . .** *(Children repeat, two thumbs up)*

Long ago, Jesus went up on a hill to pray and he sent his friends on a boat across the lake. But while they were sailing on the lake, a great big storm blew in! The thunder was crashing, and the lighting was flashing and the rain was
>   **Fallin' on the water . . .** *(Children repeat)*
>   *(Louder and more exaggerated)* **I said fallin' on the water! . . .** *(Children repeat)*
>   *(Real loud, really exaggerated)* **FALLIN' ON THE WATER!** *(Children repeat)*
>   **Huh, huh, bad! . . .** *(Children repeat, two thumbs down)*

So they were scared! And then, they looked and saw what they thought was a ghost and it was
>   **Walkin' on the water . . .**
>   **I said walkin' on the water! . . .**
>   **WALKIN' ON THE WATER!**
>   **Huh, huh, bad! . . .** *(Children repeat, two thumbs down)*

But it wasn't a ghost! It was Jesus! And he said, "Guys, don't be scared, it's just me, Jesus!"
And Peter said, "Oh, yeah! Well if it's really you, then tell me to join you!"
"Come on down!" said Jesus.
So Peter jumped out of the boat and he was

> *Standin' on the water . . .*
> *I said standin' on the water! . . .*
> *STANDIN' ON THE WATER!*
> *Huh, huh, yeah! . . . (Children repeat, two thumbs up)*

And Peter started walking to Jesus and as he did he was . . .

> *Walkin' on the water . . .*
> *I said walkin' on the water! . . .*
> *WALKIN' ON THE WATER!*
> *Huh, huh, yeah! . . . (Children repeat, two thumbs up)*

But then, Peter saw the big waves and he heard the loud wind and he stared to get scared! And when he started to get scared, he started to doubt, and when he started to doubt, he started to sink. And he was

> *Sinkin' in the water . . .*
> *I said sinkin' in the water! . . .*
> *SINKIN' IN THE WATER!*
> *Huh, huh, bad! . . . (Children repeat, two thumbs down)*

So he yelled out to Jesus, "Help me! I'm gonna die!"
And Jesus took his hand and helped him to his feet and said, "My friend, why did you ever doubt?" and together they went back to the boat. As they did they were

> *Walkin' on the water . . .*
> *I said walkin' on the water! . . .*
> *WALKIN' ON THE WATER!*
> *Huh, huh, yeah! . . . (Children repeat, two thumbs up)*

When they got to the boat the storm stopped and the disciples were so amazed they started

> *A-worshipin' a-Jesus . . .*
> *I said a-worshipin' a-Jesus! . . .*
> *WORSHIPIN' A-JESUS!*
> *Huh, huh, yeah! . . . (Children repeat, two thumbs up)*

Kids, let's pretend that we're walking on the water with Peter and Jesus! First, we have to climb over the edge of the boat . . . and jump down . . . and now, look, we're standing on the water! Cool! . . . Jump up and down on the water! . . . Do a little dance . . . This water is as strong as the floor!

OK, step over that wave that's coming . . . And look around. Do you see the big waves? Are you getting scared? . . . Show me how scared Peter was when he saw those big waves! . . .

Then, he started sinking in the water! OK, everyone sink . . . Oh no, let's call out to Jesus. "Help us Jesus!" Ready? "HELP US JESUS!"

OK, who wants to pretend to be Jesus? *(choose one student to be Jesus)* . . . All right, go and pull someone up, rescue them from sinking! . . . Now someone else! . . . Help all of them, Jesus! Hurry! . . .

OK everyone, let's walk back to the boat . . . And climb over the side . . . And let's all say, "Thank you Jesus!". . . "THANK YOU JESUS!"

Repeat the sinking and rescuing again if you want to give other children the chance to pretend to be Jesus. (You could even have half of the class be Jesus if you wish.) Then discuss how Jesus still helps us today. **"Peter was in trouble. Do bad things sometimes happen to you? Do you need Jesus' help sometimes too? How do we call out to Jesus today? Does Jesus love us and care about our problems? Does he help us? Let's all say a prayer to Jesus and thank him for helping us in hard times today."**

End with prayer.

Summary

The night was dark and the clouds were gray
And Jesus was tired from working all day;
    But instead of sleeping he went on a hill
    To pray to his Father;
    And to be quiet
        And still.

Well, the friends of Jesus were also awake,
And they'd taken a boat to sail on the lake.
But while they were sailing, and to their surprise,
A terrible storm came and covered the skies!

The water was spraying and they couldn't stay warm!
And the men were all frightened and afraid of the storm!
And none of them thought they could get to the coast,
Especially when they saw what they thought was a ghost!
    That came closer and closer and walked on the sea,
    And all of those men were as scared as can be!

But it wasn't a ghost, it was Jesus instead.
And while they were shaking, he called out and said,
"My friends, it's just me! So don't be afraid!"
Then he told Pete to join him and Peter obeyed.
But then, when he saw all those waves on the sea
Peter was scared!
    Oh, as scared as can be!

And when he got scared, Peter started to think
That he wouldn't survive!
    Then he started to sink!
"Jesus, please save me!" he yelled in the night.
Then Jesus helped Peter and Pete was all right.
Yes, Jesus came quickly when Peter called out,
    But Jesus said, "Peter, oh, why did you doubt?"

Then they climbed in the boat and the storm went away,
And the disciples all worshiped their Savior that day.

Chapter 18

Jesus Sends the Demon Away

BASED ON: Matthew 17:14-21; Mark 9:14-29; and Luke 9:37-43

BIG IDEA: Through his powerful prayer and faith, Jesus was able to cast out demons. In this story, he frees a little boy from demon possession.

BACKGROUND: As Peter, James, and John came down the mountain after the Transfiguration, they encountered a large crowd. Within the crowd were a number of religious experts arguing with the other disciples. Apparently, when Jesus' followers were unable to cast out a demon, their authority was brought into question.

Jesus became exasperated by the lack of faith exhibited by his disciples and the possessed boy's father. At last, he freed the boy from the control of the evil spirit and taught his disciples an important lesson about the power of faith.

KEY VERSE: "'If you can?' said Jesus. 'Everything is possible for him who believes'" (Mark 9:23).

When talking about demons, you'll want to be careful not to frighten the children too much. Rather, explain to them that there are angels who turned bad a long time ago and sometimes they come into people and make those people do things they wouldn't do on their own. But God wants us to be filled up with him and not anything bad like demons.

Sometimes people shy away from using puppets because they don't feel skilled enough to open and close the puppet's mouth at the appropriate times. You can solve this problem by not having the puppet say anything to the children, but instead just lean close and whisper things in your ear. Then, you can have the puppet nod or shake its head to answer your questions.

Remember to always keep your puppet moving, even when it's not talking. This will help create the illusion that the puppet is alive.

Practice the story a few times with your puppet so that you can become comfortable with the interchanges between the two of you. Don't feel like you need to memorize the following script. Instead, when you tell the story to the children, put the script aside and tell the story in your own words.

WHAT TO SAY:	SUGGESTED PUPPET ACTION:
Boys and girls, today's story has some sad parts in it and some exciting parts! I thought I would ask a friend of mine to come out here and help me tell this story to you. His name is (insert the name of your puppet; I'll give you an example of how it could work) **Fang the Wolf!**	As you introduce the puppet, pull it out of a box or crate and hold it on your lap. Remember to keep it moving!
(To the puppet) **So, Fang, today's story is about a boy who had a demon inside him. Do you know what a demon is?**	Make your puppet nod.
You do?	Nod again.
What is it?	Have the puppet lean close and whisper in your ear.
Yes, that's right. A demon is an angel that turned bad a long time ago. And they like to hurt and frighten people!	Have him hide under your arm. He's scared!
Don't worry. It's OK. This story happened a long time ago.	Bring him back out.
Well, a boy had a demon in him. And do you know what the demon would make the boy do?	Have the puppet lean close and whisper in your ear.

Yes! He would throw the boy into water or campfires or throw him to the ground to hurt him!	Have him hide under your arm again.
Um, you can come out. This was a long time ago.	Bring him back out.
Now—oh, you want to tell me something?	Nod.
What is it?	Whisper.
No, the boy is going to be OK. Just listen. Jesus' friends, the disciples, tried to make the demon go away but—	Have him hide under your arm, interrupting you.
Um, listen, you'll have to stop hiding all the time so I can finish this story. OK?	Bring him back out, reluctantly. Nod.
Now, they tried to make the demon go away, but they couldn't do it—what's that?	Whisper.
No, they couldn't do it by themselves; they would need Jesus to send this demon away. So when Jesus came up, the boy's father—	Whisper.
Yes, the boy's father wanted the demon to go away!	Nod.
He said, "Jesus please help me if there's anything you can do!" Now, do you think Jesus was happy to hear that?	Nod.
Um, no he wasn't.	Shake your head no.
Right?	Nod.
Um, you're nodding that I'm right?	Shake your head no.
You're not?	Nod.
Now, you're confusing me!	Nod.
Listen, Jesus wasn't happy. He told the man, "Anything is possible if you believe!"	Nod.
That's right. So—what is it?	Whisper.
Well, the man said, "I do believe, Jesus, please help me overcome my doubts!"	Whisper.
That's right. He believed, but he also doubted! After all, he'd tried everything and nothing had worked!	Nod.
So, then, Jesus made the demon—	Have him hide under your arm, interrupting you.
Um, he made the demon go away.	Pull him out.
And—	Whisper.
Yes, it was a happy ending! And I'm sure that father grew in his faith when he saw the power of Jesus over that demon.	Hide!
Um, the demon was gone!	Pull him out. Nod.
Great. Kids, let's thank Fang for coming out today!	Make your puppet bow to the audience. Then, put it away again in the crate or box.

The father in this story had both faith and doubt in his heart at the same time!

This story offers you a good opportunity to share a personal story from your life about a time when you had faith in God, but you also had some doubts. Did you pray that God would help you overcome the doubts? What happened to help your faith grow stronger?

We don't need to be ashamed if we don't understand something about God or have trouble believing it. Instead we need to ask God to help us have a stronger faith, just like the man in this story did.

You could use the following ideas to review the story, or you might want to use this version rather than the whisper puppet script found above.

Today's story has lots of emotions in it! Let's see if you boys and girls can show me how a happy person looks . . . what about a sad person? . . . an angry person? . . . a surprised

person? . . . Great job! OK, Let's start this story and as I tell it, you can show me what the people felt like at different times in the story!

Jesus was up on a mountain with three of his friends. He started to get all shiny, because he was God! When the disciples saw that, they were surprised . . . and confused . . . and a little scared. . . .

But then, when they realized it was OK, they were happy . . . since they could see Jesus' power!

Then, they all went down the mountain and found a crowd of people! And some of the people were angry! . . . And some were disappointed . . . You see, a man had a son and a demon was living in the boy! That made the man sad . . . And so he had asked Jesus' friends for help, but they couldn't send the demon away! That made them feel bad and embarrassed . . .

"Please help me if there's anything you can do!" said the man.

And Jesus got angry . . . "What do you mean 'if'?" said Jesus. "Anything is possible if you truly believe!"

The man felt scared Jesus wouldn't help him . . . "I do believe!" he yelled. "Please help me overcome my doubts!"

Then Jesus told the demon to go away, and it threw the boy hard against the ground! When it did that, the people were surprised! . . .

And then the boy didn't move and the people were sad . . . because they thought the boy was dead. But then Jesus helped him to his feet and everyone was surprised . . . and happy . . . that the boy was OK and the demon was gone! And that boy's daddy was super happy . . . that Jesus had helped his son be free and helped him to grow in his faith.

The end!

Summary

A man had a son whom a demon had found,
And the demon would make the boy
    Flop on the ground!
It would throw him in water and campfires too!
And that man didn't know what on earth
    He could do!
For he'd tried all he could, and the demon just stayed.
So the man was sad and upset and afraid.

"Oh, Jesus," he said, "I need you, it's true,
Please help if there's anything
    That you can do!"
But Jesus got angry and said, "Just believe!
And then there's no limit
    To what you'll receive!"
The man said, "I do, Lord! But sometimes I doubt,
Please help send the doubting part of me out!"

Then Jesus told the demon to get out and go,
And it threw the boy hard to the ground
    Down below.
And the people said, "Oh no! The child won't survive!"
But then Jesus helped him up—
    The boy was alive!
The demon had left and his father's faith grew.
When he saw what the power of believing can do.

Chapter 19

Lazarus Comes Back to Life

BASED ON: John 11:1-45

BIG IDEA: Jesus brought Lazarus back to life in order to bring glory to God and to give the people an opportunity to believe in Jesus.

BACKGROUND: Toward the end of his life, Jesus knew that the Jewish leaders were trying to trap him. It was becoming more dangerous than ever for him to appear in public. Still, he raised Lazarus from the dead in front of lots of witnesses, revealing his power and true identity.

In the aftermath of this miracle, the Jews were so committed to extinguishing the excitement about Jesus that they planned to kill both Jesus and Lazarus (see John 12:9, 10, 17).

KEY VERSE: "Jesus said to her, 'I am the resurrection and the life. He who believes in me will live, even though he dies; and whoever lives and believes in me will never die. Do you believe this?'" (John 11:25, 26)

Contrary to what some people think, Jesus didn't raise his friend from the dead because he was sad or because he missed him. He did it specifically to bring glory to God and to give people an opportunity to believe. This point is clearly emphasized throughout the story (see John 11:4, 15, 25, 40, 42, 45). (Note that in many Bibles, a section break appears after verse 44 rather than after verse 45. This is misleading since John 11:45 is the conclusion of the story about Lazarus.)

Don't spend too much time emphasizing the death of Lazarus, but rather the power Jesus has, and the hope that we can have of rising to be with him forever when we trust in him.

Puppets can be helpful when you're telling a story that's intense or sad like this one. Puppets can help children think about difficult topics without being overly frightened or intimidated.

Here's a script to use with a whisper puppet. You don't need to make the puppet open and close its mouth; just have it whisper in your ear, nod, or shake its head.

WHAT TO SAY:	SUGGESTED PUPPET ACTION:
Kids I'd like to tell a story with my friend this morning. His name is *(insert the name of your puppet; I'll give you an example of how it could work)* **Fang the Wolf!**	As you introduce the puppet, pull it out of a box or crate and hold it on your lap. Remember to keep it moving!
(To the puppet) So, Fang, are you ready for the story?	Make your puppet nod.
Today's story is a little sad but it has a happy ending.	Make your puppet whisper to you.
What's that? You want to help tell this story?	Nod.
Well, Jesus had a friend named—	Whisper.
Um, no. Jesus' friend was not named George! He was named Lazarus!	Nod.
One day, Lazarus got very sick.	Whisper.
Um, I don't really know if he threw up. I just know he was really sick.	Nod.

So his sisters, who were named—	Whisper.
No, his sisters weren't named Betsy and Clementine!	Nod enthusiastically.
They were named Mary and Martha!	Whisper.
Yes, I'm sure.	Whisper.
No, neither of them was named George!	Nod.
Anyway, they asked Jesus to come and heal their brother, but Jesus stayed right where he was.	Whisper.
Why? Well Jesus didn't go because he wanted to do something even better than healing Lazarus—	Whisper.
Well, I'm not going to tell you right now. You'll need to listen to the rest of the story to find out.	Shake his head back and forth.
Yes, you'll have to wait.	Shake his head some more.
I'm afraid so.	Turn the puppet against your shoulder and let him shake as if he's crying.
Oh, brother.	Nod.
Anyway, after waiting for a little while, Jesus went to go see Lazarus.	Whisper.
No, not George, Lazarus!	Whisper.
Was Lazarus OK?	Nod.
Well, actually no. He was dead!	Make him hide his head; he's scared!
But don't worry. Jesus is stronger than death.	Have him come out of hiding and nod.
So Martha was sad	Turn the puppet against your shoulder and shake him as if he's crying.
And Jesus told her that he is the one who gives life forever!	Have him peek out.
"Do you believe that?" he asked her, and she said, "Yes."	Nod.
Then Mary came out and she was sad . . .	More crying and shaking.
And the people were sad . . .	More puppet tears.
And even Jesus was sad . . .	Even more.
But Jesus said—	Whisper.
No, he didn't say, "George, come out!" He said, "Lazarus, come out!"	Nod.
And his friend came out—alive!	Have him stare at you. He's surprised.
Yes, really, he was alive!	Whisper.
No, HE DIDN'T CHANGE HIS NAME TO GEORGE!	Nod.
That day lots of people trusted in Jesus!	Lots of nodding!
And Jesus brought even more fame to his Father!	More nodding!
Great. Kids, let's thank Fang for coming out today!	Make your puppet bow to the audience. Then, put it away again in the crate or box.

When telling the following sound effects story, remember to limit the number of times the children say the refrain lines so they don't get carried away and keep saying them over and over again.

STORY:	REFRAINS:
Jesus had a friend named Lazarus. One day Lazarus got very sick!	Throw! Throw! Throw-y up! Throw! Throw! Throw-y up! Throw! Throw! Throw-y up!
But when they told Jesus about it, he didn't go to see Lazarus!	Huh? Huh? Huh, what, huh? Huh? Huh? Huh, what, huh? Huh? Huh? Huh, what, huh?
You see, Jesus wanted to bring him back from the dead!	Wow. Wow. Wow-y wow! Wow. Wow. Wow-y wow! Wow. Wow. Wow-y wow!
Finally, Jesus and his friends went to see Mary and Martha, who were very sad.	Waa! Waa! Waa-y waa! Waa! Waa! Waa-y waa! Waa! Waa! Waa-y waa!
Because their brother Lazarus had died.	Sad. Sad. Sad-y sad. Sad. Sad. Sad-y sad. Sad. Sad. Sad-y sad.
But Jesus said, "Do you believe I can give new life?" And Martha said, "I believe that you are the Son of God!"	Son. Son. Son of God! Son. Son. Son of God! Son. Son. Son of God!
Then they took Jesus to the tomb, and Jesus cried.	Boo. Boo. Boo-hoo boo. Boo. Boo. Boo-hoo boo. Boo. Boo. Boo-hoo boo.
The people who saw him cry knew that Jesus had really loved his friend Lazarus.	Friend. Friend. Friendy friend. Friend. Friend. Friendy friend. Friend. Friend. Friendy friend.
Then Jesus said, "Roll away the stone!" But Martha said, "He's been dead for four days! By now he's all stinky!"	Stink. Stink. Stinky guy! Stink. Stink. Stinky guy! Stink. Stink. Stinky guy!
But Jesus told them to do it anyway, and when they did, Jesus yelled, "Lazarus, come on out!"	Come, come, come on out! Come, come, come on out! Come, come, come on out!
And Lazarus did! He was alive! Jesus had brought him back to life!	Back, back, back to life! Back, back, back to life! Back, back, back to life!
And he wasn't stinky at all!	Smell. Smell. Smelling good! Smell. Smell. Smelling good! Smell. Smell. Smelling good!
When the people saw it, they were amazed	Whoa. Whoa. Whoa-y whoa. Whoa. Whoa. Whoa-y whoa. Whoa. Whoa. Whoa-y whoa.
And believed in Jesus.	Son. Son. Son of God! Son. Son. Son of God! Son. Son. Son of God!
The end!	Hip! Hip! Hip hooray! Hip! Hip! Hip hooray! Hip! Hip! Hip hooray!

Summary

Mary was sad for her brother was sick,
So she sent word to Jesus, "Hurry up and come quick!
Come heal my poor brother or he might soon be dead!"
But Jesus stayed right where he was instead!
      (Now Jesus had a plan, so don't be too worried,
      And his plan wouldn't work if he rushed or he hurried.)

At last Jesus left with his friends by his side.
And he went to see Lazarus, but Lazarus had died.
So the people were sad and the people were crying,
For they knew Jesus could have stopped Lazarus from dying!
      "Why didn't you come?" they said,
      "You shouldn't have stayed!"
But Jesus said, "Show me where the body was laid."

Then Martha said, "Jesus, our brother is dead,
So he won't smell too pretty, but stinky instead!"
Still, they rolled back the stone and Jesus let out a shout,
      "Lazarus, my friend!
      I say, Lazarus come out!"

Then the people saw Lazarus step out of the cave
That had served for the last couple days as his grave!
And the people were shocked and the people were dazed;
And all of the folks who had watched were amazed!
      And many of them trusted in Jesus that hour,
      When they saw the incredible display of his power.

You see Jesus wasn't mean when he waited to come.
He wasn't being naughty or pouty or dumb.
Jesus could have healed him when he was sick, but instead
He did what was harder and brought him back from the dead!

Chapter 20

No Longer Blind!

BASED ON: John 9

BIG IDEA: Jesus healed a man who had been born blind. Then Jesus taught about the importance of his mission of curing inner, spiritual blindness.

BACKGROUND: The Pharisees refused to believe in Jesus even when the evidence was overwhelming. They rejected him because they were spiritually blind, *but they thought they weren't.* Only those who acknowledge their spiritual blindness can ever see spiritual truth and believe in Jesus.

Once again, Jesus heals on the Sabbath day, enraging the legalistic Pharisees. In the aftermath of the healing, the man who was born blind gives a compelling testimony to them and becomes a follower of Christ.

KEY VERSE: "He replied, 'Whether he is a sinner or not, I don't know. One thing I do know. I was blind but now I see!'" (John 9:25)

The disciples thought that if something bad happened to you (such as being born blind) that God must be punishing you for your sins (see John 9:3, 5, 34).

Jesus explained that sometimes God has something entirely different in mind when he allows bad things to occur.

Here's a way to tell this story with simple props. Before class, gather the props and put them in a special crate or colorful cloth bag.

Once, Jesus met a man who was blind *(pull out the eyeglasses).* **So, Jesus spit on the ground** *(a big bottle of water labeled "SPIT!")* **took some dirt** *(hold up a clump of dirt)* **and made mud** *(go ahead, make some mud).* **Then, he put it on the man's eyes** *(smear some on the eyeglasses)* **and told him to go and wash in the pool of Siloam** *(a bowl of water).*

So, he did *(dip the glasses in the water and wipe off the mud).* **And then, he could see!** *(put the glasses on and say, "Whoa, dude!").*

At first his friends and family couldn't believe it was really him! "It's me!" he said. "But how?" they asked. "You used to be blind!"

(As you go through this routine again and again, repeat the procedures with the props.)

And he told them how Jesus had spit . . . and took some dirt . . . and made some mud . . . and put it on his eyes . . . and then, how he'd washed off in the pool . . . *(put the glasses on and say, "Whoa, dude!").*

Then, the leaders heard about it! They called him in and asked him the same questions, and he told them the same thing: how Jesus mixed some spit . . . with some dirt . . . and made some mud . . . and put it on his eyes . . . and then, how he'd washed off in a pool . . . and he could see! . . . *(put the glasses on and say, "Whoa, dude!").*

They were amazed that Jesus had healed him like that, but they didn't want to follow Jesus even when the man said, "I once was blind, but now I see!"

They refused to believe in Jesus, but that man believed. And he worshiped Jesus because Jesus is the Son of God!

Everyone who sees clearly knows that Jesus is the Son of God! *(put the glasses on and say, "Whoa, dude!").*

The end!

This story gives us a good example of how to witness. The man whom Jesus healed didn't know a lot of deep theological answers, but he did know that Jesus had helped him and done something for him that no one else could ever do. When we tell people about Jesus, it can be that simple as we share how Jesus saved us.

For the following story, each time through the refrain, get a little faster. Repeat the refrain several times each time it comes up.

One day Jesus was talking with his friends. They met a man who couldn't see. He'd never been able to see anything his whole life! Close your eyes, kids, to find out what it would be like to be blind! . . . Is it dark when you close your eyes? . . . That's what it was like for this man all the time! OK, you can open your eyes.

Well, Jesus' friends thought maybe the man had done something bad and God was punishing him. Or maybe his parents had done something bad. Like stealing . . . or hurting someone . . . or lying all the time!

But Jesus said, no, God doesn't act like that. Instead, God let that man be born blind so something wonderful could happen that day.

Then Jesus spit on the ground and made some mud. Then he put it on the man's eyes and then Jesus told him to go and wash in a special pool.

(Say with rhythm)

> *He spit on the ground* (Pretend to spit by emphasizing the "p" when you say spit)
> *And he made some mud . . .* (Rub your hands together)
> *And he put it on his eyes . . .* (Put your hands up to your eyes)
> *So that he could see!* (Pull your hands away and open your eyes)

Let's do that together . . . *(Repeat, inviting the children to join in)*

Well, the man did what Jesus said, and when he did the man could see!

So everyone was amazed. Show me how surprised everyone was! . . . His friends and family couldn't believe it!

"You're someone else," they said.

"No I'm not! It's me!"

"But how can you see?" they said.

And he told them, "I met a man named Jesus:

> *He spit on the ground . . .*
> *And he made some mud . . .*
> *And he put it on my eyes . . .*
> *So that I could see! . . .*
> *(repeat together)*

But some of the leaders thought Jesus shouldn't have helped that man because he did it on the day of rest. Besides, they could hardly believe that this man had been born unable to see. So they asked him, and he told them what had happened:

> *He spit on the ground . . .*
> *And he made some mud . . .*
> *And he put it on my eyes . . .*
> *So that I could see! . . .*
> *(repeat)*

But they didn't believe him! So they asked his parents and then they asked him again. Each time the man said, "I was blind, but now I see!"

"But how did Jesus help you see?" they asked.

"I told you before," he said:

> He spit on the ground . . .
> And he made some mud . . .
> And he put it on my eyes . . .
> So that I could see! . . .
> *(repeat)*

"Then I went and washed like he told me to," he said, "and then I could see! Only God can heal someone like that! Jesus must be one of God's helpers!"

But those men didn't like Jesus so they said, "Huh! He's not really helping God."

"Then how could he heal me?" the guy said. "I'm his follower now; maybe you want to come follow him too?"

But those men didn't want anything to do with Jesus. And so, they said mean things to the man—but he didn't care. Because now he was a follower of Jesus. And he told all the people he met:

> He spit on the ground . . .
> And he made some mud . . .
> And he put it on my eyes . . .
> So that I could see! . . .
> *(repeat)*

He believed in Jesus and worshiped him! His eyes and his heart had both been blind, but Jesus brought light and healing to them both!

The end!

Summary

Jesus made mud with some spit and some dirt
And he put it on a blind man's eyes.
And when he washed up (I don't think that it hurt)
Well, suddenly to his surprise,
He could see birdies and freckles and clouds!
And he could see flowers growing up from the earth!
>   But the leaders could hardly believe he was healed
>   When they heard he'd been blind since the day of his birth!

So they were upset, as you might have guessed,
Because Jesus made mud on a day
When they thought that people should just take a rest.
"No more making of mud!" they would say.

So they asked that man again and again
How he'd been healed and was able to see.
"I told you before," he answered the men,
"Jesus smeared some mud onto me!"

But they didn't like Jesus so they wouldn't believe,
"But how? Tell us how!" they commanded.
"For Jesus isn't holy, he's here to deceive
So now tell us the truth!" they demanded.

And the man who'd been blind just sighed and replied.
>   "I told you before and I'll say it once more:
>   I was blind, but now I see colors galore!
>   What more can I tell you? What more can I say?
>   The man of God came and healed me today!"

Chapter 21

Many, Many Languages

BASED ON: Acts 2

BIG IDEA: At Pentecost, God's Spirit filled the believers and the Christian church was born.

BACKGROUND: After Jesus ascended into Heaven, the disciples waited in Jerusalem for the arrival of the promised Holy Spirit. At the Pentecost holiday, 50 days after Passover (and subsequently 50 days after the institution of the Lord's Supper), the Holy Spirit arrived. He filled the believers with his presence and miraculously allowed them to speak in (and be heard in) other languages.

    Peter preached his first sermon that day and thousands became followers of Christ. The Christian church had begun! That day about 3000 people responded to Peter's sermon, believed in Christ, and were baptized.

KEY VERSE: "Those who accepted his message were baptized, and about three thousand were added to their number that day" (Acts 2:41).

While Christians agree that the Holy Spirit filled and empowered the early believers in a supernatural way at Pentecost, different churches and denominations interpret the idea of speaking in tongues differently. Some believe that Christians today still speak in tongues; others think that this gift of the Spirit was reserved for the early Christian church. Be sensitive to the denominational distinctives of your church and the background of your students when teaching on this topic.

Today's story is very exciting! It's about when God's Spirit came down from Heaven to live in the hearts of his people!

Long ago, after Jesus came back to life from the dead, he went to live with God in Heaven. But before he left, he told his friends that he would send the Holy Spirit to be with them.

And so, they waited and prayed, and then one day, they heard the sound of a great big wind. What do you think that wind sounded like? . . . Oh, no. It was louder than that . . . even louder! . . . That's more like it!

And the men didn't know what was going on. Because when they talked, they all spoke in other languages! Have you ever heard someone talk in another language? What did it sound like? . . . Everyone talk in another language right now and let's see what it sounds like. Ready? Go! . . . Wow! It sure is hard to hear what people are saying . . .

And then, something even more interesting happened. Little flickers of fire appeared on the people's heads! That's right! But don't worry, it didn't burn the people. Instead, it just showed that God's Spirit was living in their hearts!

Well, when the people outside heard that loud wind—let's hear it again . . . and heard all those people talking in so many different languages—go ahead . . . they were confused. Especially because they could each hear people talking in the language that they understood!

Then Peter stood up and told the people about Jesus. That day more than 3000 people believed in Jesus and were baptized!

The church grew and God's Spirit filled the hearts of his people!

Below is a fun way to encourage children to make sound effects that relate to this story. The children will become louder and softer as you direct them. Say something like this: **"OK kids, I want you to make the sounds for this story! When I raise my hand, get louder and faster. When I lower my hand, get softer and slower. Let's warm up and practice by saying 'Cool!'"**

Start with your hand in the middle, raise it higher slowly, and then slowly lower it. Raise it again; then lower it again. Try it a little faster, then slowly again. Be a little silly. Then, put your hand at your side to indicate to the children when to be quiet. **"Don't forget that when I put my hand down by my side you'll need to be quiet again!"**

WHAT TO SAY:	SUGGESTED ACTION:
After Jesus went back to Heaven, his friends got together at a house to pray. "We love Jesus," they would say. Let's say that like we're really excited! "WE LOVE JESUS! WE LOVE JESUS! . . . " *(Repeat it with them several times as you move your hand around.)*	Hold your hand in the middle, and then raise it up high. Move it up and down a few times if you wish.
But sometimes they would pray it quietly . . .	Lower your hand. *(Drop your hand to your side.)*
One day, as they were praying, they heard what sounded like a great big wind! "WHOOSH! WHOOSH!"	Hold your hand in the middle; then raise it up high.
It was really loud!	Higher.
Really, really loud!	Even higher!
And then it went away.	*(Drop your hand to your side.)*
And when they talked they were talking in other languages! Pretend to talk in another language, ready? "BLAB. BLAB. BLAB."	Start with your hand in the middle, raise it up and down a bit. Have fun with it! Be a little silly! *(Drop your hand to your side.)*
Soon a crowd formed outside the house. Sometimes they were pushing each other, maybe even stepping on each other's toes! "AHH! AHH!"	Start with your hand in the middle, raise it up. Lower it. Have fun with it.
But when they heard all the talking in other languages, they became quiet so they could listen better.	Lower your hand. *(Drop your hand to your side.)*
Then some people started shouting because they thought Jesus' friends had been partying too much! Let's hear you shout! "HEY! HEY! HEY!"	Hold your hand in the middle; then raise it up high.
But Peter quieted down the crowd.	Lower your hand.
He explained that God's Spirit had come into them. Then he told the people about Jesus. Some of the people listening were sad and started to cry because they were sorry Jesus had to die! "WAA!"	Raise it up even higher! *(Drop your hand to your side.)*
They cried really loud!	Higher.
Even louder!	Higher.
Louder!	Even higher! *(Drop your hand to your side.)*
Then, Peter told them to trust in Jesus and be baptized. And that day 3000 people jumped in the water to be baptized. There was a lot of splashing! "SPLASHY! SPLASHY!"	Start your hand really low. Raise it and lower it as desired.
Sometimes there was a lot of splashing!	Higher.
Then, the people cheered because they were so happy to be saved. "YEA! YEA!"	Higher.
And they said, "We love Jesus!" Ready? "WE LOVE JESUS! WE LOVE JESUS!"	Even higher!
They said it really loud because they meant it!	Highest position of all!
The end! Good job!	

Summary

The people of God had seen Jesus rise
Up to Heaven and float from the earth to the skies.
And they knew he had promised that soon he would send
The Spirit, the Comforter, the heavenly Friend.

So they waited and watched and together they stayed
Upstairs at the house where they worshiped and prayed.
'Til one day they heard a great rush and a roar;
It was louder than any wind they'd heard before!
      But it wasn't a breeze, it was the really the Lord!

God's Spirit had come, and when they stood up to shout,
They didn't understand all the words that came out!
For they all spoke in languages they hadn't yet learned
And on top of their heads fires flickered and burned!
      (But they didn't get hurt for God's Spirit was there
      And not little campfires roasting their hair!)

The people nearby didn't know what to do!
They didn't realize Jesus' words had come true.
Then Peter stood up and he shouted and said,
That Jesus had come back to life from the dead!

And that very day as he spoke to the crowd
Thousands of people started crying out loud!
And as Peter told them all God's special Word,
About 3000 people believed what they heard!

Chapter 22

Peter and John Help a Man Walk

BASED ON: Acts 3, 4

BIG IDEA: Peter and John boldly and unashamedly taught people about Jesus. They weren't highly trained theologians, but their message and ministry were inspired and guided by the Holy Spirit.

BACKGROUND: As the early church grew, Peter and John boldly shared the message of salvation in Christ. One afternoon, on their way to pray at the Temple, Peter healed a man who had been born lame. The miracle caused quite a stir in Jerusalem. As Peter explained that the miracle-working power came from the risen Jesus, the Sadducees bristled with anger and indignation since they didn't believe in the resurrection of the dead.

After a night in jail, Peter and John returned to meet with the other believers to pray for boldness and clarity in their witnessing. Immediately, God answered their prayer.

KEY VERSE: "Then they called them in again and commanded them not to speak or teach at all in the name of Jesus. But Peter and John replied, 'Judge for yourselves whether it is right in God's sight to obey you rather than God. For we cannot help speaking about what we have seen and heard'" (Acts 4:18-20).

As you read this story in the Bible, you'll come across a few terms that might be unfamiliar. The Sadducees were a rich and influential group of religious leaders who didn't believe in the resurrection or immortal souls, so it's obvious why they didn't like Peter and John talking about Jesus coming back to life. The Sanhedrin was a group of important leaders similar to a supreme court.

Remind the children that Peter and John didn't have the power to heal anybody. All their healing power came through Jesus.

I'm going to teach you something to say and something special to do when I tell today's story! When I say <u>money</u> we'll all pretend that we're weighing a bag full of gold in our hands and say, "Please, please, I need some cash!" Let's try it: "PLEASE, PLEASE, I NEED SOME CASH!"

And whenever I talk about <u>feet</u> we'll throw out our hands and say, "Ta-da!" Ready, let's practice: "TA-DA!"

And finally, whenever I talk about <u>Jesus</u>, we'll put a fist up in the air and say really loudly, "God is powerful and on our side!" "GOD IS POWERFUL AND ON OUR SIDE!"

OK, let's start the story!

Long ago there was a man who couldn't walk! The only job he could get was sitting by the side of the road and asking people for <u>money</u>. *(Please, please, I need some cash!)*

So, Peter and John were on their way to pray at the worship place when they met the man. And of course he asked them for some <u>money</u>. *(Please, please, I need some cash!)*

Well, they didn't have any money, but they did have the power of <u>Jesus</u>! *(God is powerful and on our side!)*

Peter told the man, "Look at me!" And the man thought that for sure he was going to get some <u>money</u>. *(Please, please, I need some cash!)*

But Peter said, "We don't have silver and we don't have gold, but we do have the power of <u>Jesus</u>!" *(God is powerful and on our side!)*

And then he said, "In the name of Jesus, I tell you, get up and walk!" And Peter took the guy's hand and helped him to his <u>feet</u>. *(Ta-da!)* And immediately his legs and ankles were healed and strong! And he could use his <u>feet</u>! *(Ta-da!)*

And he started jumping, and leaping, and praising <u>Jesus</u>! *(God is powerful and on our side!)*

Everyone who saw it was amazed that he could stand up on his own two <u>feet</u>! *(Ta-da!)*

And let me tell you, that man was happy because he would never again have to sit there and ask for <u>money</u>. *(Please, please, I need some cash!)*

He was very thankful to Peter and John, but he was even more thankful for the power of <u>Jesus,</u> *(God is powerful and on our side!)* who had helped him walk and use his <u>feet</u>! *(Ta-da!)*

The end.

As you and a partner lead the following story, one of you reads the words while the other leads the actions. As each action is performed, the students will mirror the action back to you. Practice this story a few times before class to make sure the pace is smooth and the pauses are long enough. The empty spaces that appear after certain lines are simply there to break up the story and make it easier for you to find and keep your place.

WHAT TO SAY:	WHAT TO DO:
One day, Peter and John were walking to the temple.	Walk in place.
They wanted to go and pray to God!	Fold hands in prayer.
They met a man who asked them for money.	Hold out your hand.
The man couldn't walk because his legs didn't work.	Grab your legs and make yourself walk by using your hands.
So every day his friends would carry him there,	Pretend to carry something very heavy!
Set him down,	Drop it.
And he would beg people for money.	Hold out your hand again.
But Peter didn't have any money.	Shake your head "no." Fold out your pocket to show that it's empty.
But he did have something else!	Hold up your hand as if to say, "Aha!"
"Look at me!" said Peter	Turn your head and stare at someone.
So the man did.	Turn your head and stare in the other direction.
He told the man that he could stand up and walk	Point to your chest. As if to say, who me?
Because Jesus had healed him.	Point up to Heaven.
Then, Peter took the guy's hand.	Reach out your hand.
And he helped him to his feet.	Jump and look surprised that you're standing up!
For the first time in his life he stood up!	Stand tall!
He started to walk around!	Walk in place.
And jump up and down!	Jump.
And dance all over the place.	Dance around.
He started praising God!	Throw up your arms to praise God!
Then, he went with Peter and John into the temple to pray.	Fold your hands.
When people heard what had happened,	Cup your hand behind your ear.

They rushed out to see for themselves!	Run in place!
And they saw the man standing there, hugging Peter and John!	Hug someone.
And the people were amazed!	Look totally surprised.
Peter told everyone Jesus had healed the man!	Point up to Heaven.
Well, some of the leaders were angry.	Hands on your hips. Look angry.
They arrested Peter and John and tied them up!	Hands together like they're tied up.
They asked them lots of questions to see how they helped the man, but Peter and John just kept talking about Jesus!	Point up to Heaven.
The men got angry,	Make a fist, look angry.
But didn't know what else to do.	Shrug your shoulders.
Finally they had to let Peter and John go home.	Walk in place.
Peter and John hurried to meet the other believers.	Run in place.
And together they all prayed.	Fold your hands.
And asked God to make them brave!	Hands on your hips.
Then, the building they were in shook!	Tip back and forth like you're in an earthquake.
And when it was over, they were braver than ever in sharing God's story!	Hands on your hips. Nod. Smile.
God had answered their prayer,	Fold your hands.
Through the power of Jesus!	Point up to Heaven.
The end!	Bow and take a seat.

Summary

Peter and John met a man by the road
And that man couldn't walk or carry a load.
So he sat there and waited and asked folks for money.
So that he could buy bread or nachos or honey.

So when Peter and John approached on the road
He asked them for silver, or maybe for gold.
But they didn't have money, instead Peter said,
    "In the name of Jesus pick up your bed,
    Stand up!
    You are healed!
    Get up on your feet!"
So the guy jumped up and did a dance on the street!
The people nearby didn't know what to say
When that man started walking and leaping that day!

So they asked Peter and John how they'd helped that man,
And they said, "We can't heal people, but Jesus can!
    His power, not ours, is the power we use
    And that power can be inside you if you choose
    To just trust in Jesus and never refuse
    To believe in his story and share the good news!"
So the story of Jesus spread all over the land.
And many believed when God healed that man!

Chapter 23

An African Man Believes

BASED ON: Acts 8:26-40

BIG IDEA: Philip, an early missionary to non-Jews, witnessed to the treasurer of Queen Candace of Ethiopia. The man trusted in Christ and became the first recorded Christian convert from the continent of Africa.

BACKGROUND: Philip was one of the men chosen to distribute food to the Grecian Jewish widows (see Acts 6:3-5). Then (after the martyrdom of his coworker, Stephen), he traveled to Samaria and taught there (Acts 8:1-25). Though most Jews hated Samaritans, Philip didn't.

      In this story, we hear of Philip responding to the Spirit's urging and finding himself in a position to witness to the treasurer of the country of Ethiopia. The man believed, was baptized, and took the message of Christ back with him to Africa.

      In each of these cases, Philip stepped across racial and ethnic lines to witness to people with whom many Jews wouldn't even have spoken.

KEY VERSE: "Then Philip began with that very passage of Scripture and told him the good news about Jesus" (Acts 8:35).

The man from Africa was a eunuch, but all you will need to do to explain his job to your students is to mention that he watched over the gold, or that he was the treasurer to a queen in Africa.

In this story both Peter and the Ethiopian man believed God's Word and responded to it. You might wish to share a personal story about a time in your life when you *didn't* listen to God's Word. What happened? What did you learn? What discovery about God, or about yourself, did you make? How did that change your life?

Long ago there was a man named Philip. His job was to give food to women who were hungry *(Yummy, yummy! Want some food? Yummy! Want some food?)***.**

One day, he heard a voice from Heaven *(Listen, Philip! I'm talking to you!)***. The voice told Philip to go to the desert** *(Whew, baby! It's hot out here!)***. And so Philip obeyed and did just what he was told.**

When he got to the desert, God's Spirit spoke to him *(Listen, Philip! I'm talking to you!)* **and told him to go over by a chariot, which is a special cart pulled by horses** *(Neigh! Neigh! I want some hay!)***.**

When he got there, he met a man from Africa *(Whew, baby! It's hot out here!)***. The man's job was to help guard the treasures of the queen!** *(Shiny, shiny treasures! I like them very much!)*

The man from Africa was reading from the Bible and Philip asked him if he understood what he was reading. *(Listen, Mister! I'm talking to you!)*

And he said, "How can I unless someone tells me what the story means?"

So, Philip—the guy who handed out food to the hungry women—*(Yummy, yummy! Want some food? Yummy! Want some food?)* **—climbed up into the chariot** *(Neigh! Neigh! I want some hay!)* **and explained all about Jesus!** *(Hip, hip hooray!)*

Well, the man believed in Jesus *(Hip, hip hooray!)* **and soon they came to a lake and the man said, "What's to stop me from being baptized?"** *(Goin' under. Comin' up a brand new guy!)*

And Philip was like, "Nothing, dude! Hop in the water!"

So he did and Philip baptized him! *(Goin' under. Comin' up a brand new guy!)*

Then, God's Spirit *(Listen, Philip! I'm talking to you!)* **took Philip away to tell more people**

about Jesus, and the man from Africa *(Whew, baby! It's hot out here!)* went back home, with his heart full of joy *(Hip, hip hooray!)* because he had been baptized *(Goin' under. Comin' up a brand new person!)* and had learned to trust in Jesus *(Hip, hip hooray!)*.

The end!

To review that both Philip and the treasurer from Africa heard and responded to God's Word, you could teach the children the following refrains, sung to the tune of "Are You Sleeping?"

Philip listened.
Philip listened.
To God's Word!
To God's Word!
And whatever God said,
And whatever God said,
Philip heard.
Philip heard.

[The] treasurer trusted,
[The] treasurer trusted,
In God's Word!
In God's Word!
And whatever God said,
And whatever God said,
[The] treasurer heard.
[The] treasurer heard.

Here's another way to tell this story by acting it out together as a class.

Boys and girls, let's pretend that we are serving food like Philip did! All the boys, you be Philip, and the girls, you pretend that you're really hungry! . . . Hungrier than that! . . . Even hungrier! . . . And boys, hand them some food! Is it heavy? Are you carrying a big tray of food? . . . I wonder if anyone has popcorn? . . . Corn on the cob? . . . Corn on the dog . . . You know, corn dogs! OK, girls, go ahead and eat up your food . . . Mmm . . .

Then, God told Philip to go to the desert! He went right away! Everybody, let's go to the desert! . . . And we're walking through the desert . . . Is it hot? . . . Whew! . . . Don't get bitten by a scorpion!

Then, God's Spirit told him to go over by the chariot, so he did . . . Let's go over by the chariot! . . . He heard the horses . . . NEIGH! NEIGH!

Then, the man invited Philip up into the chariot to tell him about the Bible. Let's climb up into the chariot . . . and sit down . . .

And let's ride in the chariot . . . BUMPITY, BUMPITY, BUMPITY BUMP. BUMPITY, BUMPITY, BUMP!

Then Philip told the man about Jesus and the man believed. So, as they rode along, he saw some water and wanted to be baptized. So, they climbed down . . . Walked over to the water . . . Stepped into the water . . . Is it cold? Brr!

And Philip baptized his new friend! Then the man was very happy. Show me how happy he was . . . I'll bet he was even happier than that . . . Even happier! . . .

Then God's Spirit sent Philip away: *(waving)* BYE, BYE PHILIP! . . . And the man from Africa climbed out of the water . . . walked back to the chariot . . . Maybe he even petted the horses . . . NEIGH! NEIGH! . . . climbed aboard . . . sat down . . . and returned home to tell people about his two new friends—Philip and Jesus!

As he rode really fast in his chariot . . . BUMPITY, BUMPITY, BUMPITY BUMP. BUMPITY, BUMPITY, BUMP!

The end!

Summary

Philip was faithful.
He listened to God,
He did what God told him even when it was odd!
Like the day that God told him
To go near a road
In the desert! Yet Philip did what he was told.

And he heard a man reading
In a chariot nearby,
(He was reading aloud). So Philip called to the guy.
        "Sir, do you understand
        All those words that you read?"
And the man said, "Come help me!" and Philip agreed.

Phillip told him of Jesus
And that man was excited.
He trusted in Jesus and his faith was ignited!
Then Philip baptized him,
And joy filled his heart.
And Philip went away; God made him depart.

Now that man lived in Africa
And worked for the queen.
He watched over her treasures that would glisten and gleam.
But he'd found the best treasure
Anyone can receive
When he trusted in Jesus and began to believe.

Chapter 24

Paul Meets Jesus

BASED ON: Acts 9:1-22

BIG IDEA: God saved Saul on the road to Damascus. Ironically, he became free (becoming a Christian) on his way to imprison others (who were already Christians)!

BACKGROUND: After the stoning of Stephen, persecution against the early Christian church spread rapidly. Saul of Tarsus was an enthusiastic Pharisee dedicated to imprisoning Christians (who were at this point in history called Followers of the Way). On the road to Damascus, Saul had a dramatic conversion experience and became one of the very people he had so violently persecuted.

God had chosen Saul as his messenger to kings, Jews, and Gentiles. Saul, later called Paul (Acts 13:9), wrote a third of the New Testament.

KEY VERSE: "Yet Saul grew more and more powerful and baffled the Jews living in Damascus by proving that Jesus is the Christ" (Acts 9:22).

It's noteworthy that when Jesus appeared to Saul, he didn't ask, "Why do you persecute my church?" He asked, "Why do you persecute me?" (Acts 9:4). Why? Because the church *is* the body of Christ (see Ephesians 5:23, Colossians 1:24)!

Saul was later called Paul. Calling him Saul during this story might be confusing to your students who might think of the Old Testament king by that name. It would probably be less confusing to just call him Paul, as I've done in the stories below. Do whichever you think is best.

For this first story, you'll need:

• two Barbie dolls, action figures, or dolls (one of them will represent Jesus)
• flashlight

Decide which of the dolls will represent Paul and which one will be Ananias. Read through the story before class a couple of times, practicing it aloud so you won't need to look at the script as you tell the story to your class.

WHAT TO SAY:	SUGGESTED ACTION:
Paul didn't like Christians.	Shake Paul's head "no."
He wanted to put them in jail!	Nod his head.
He was mean!	Shake him like he's mean!
One day he was walking along the road	Make Paul walk along the road.
When he saw a really bright light!	Turn on the flashlight. Shine it directly in Paul's face.
He fell to the ground.	Make Paul drop facedown.
And he heard a voice from Heaven. "Paul! Why are you attacking me?"	Wiggle the flashlight as you make Jesus speak to Paul.
And Paul said, "Who are you?"	Make him cower, he's scared.
"I'm Jesus!" the voice said. "Now go, and obey what I say!"	Wiggle the flashlight as you make Jesus speak to Paul.
Then, the light went away.	Turn off the flashlight.
But when Paul got up to go, he couldn't see anything because the light had blinded him!	Make Paul stumble around, get confused, walk in the wrong direction. Have fun with it. Be a little silly.

Then, the Lord spoke to a Christian man named Ananias who lived in a nearby city.	Turn on the flashlight again. Shine it at Ananias.
Ananias was asleep at the time.	Lay Ananias down.
And God spoke to him, "Go to the man named Paul and place your hands on him. He's blind and when you do that, I'll heal him!"	Wiggle the flashlight as you make Jesus speak to Ananias.
But Ananias was scared and began to shake.	Shake him.
He knew Paul didn't like Christians and wanted to put them in jail! But God told him, "Go! I've chosen him!"	Wiggle the flashlight as you make Jesus speak to Ananias.
So, Ananias went.	Turn off the flashlight, make Ananias walk.
Until he came to the place Paul was staying.	Pick up Paul.
He placed his hands on Paul.	Put Ananias's hands on Paul
And Ananias said, "Jesus, the one who appeared to you in the road—	Turn on the flashlight, shine it around.
Has sent me here to heal you so God's Spirit can fill up your heart! Brother Paul, receive your sight!" And when he said that, something like scales fell from Paul's eyes.	Make Paul wipe his eyes.
And Paul was healed!	Dance Paul around to show how happy he is!
Right away Paul began to tell people about Jesus.	Turn on the flashlight and let Paul hold it.
And share the good news of Jesus with everyone he met.	Shine the flashlight out toward the children.
The end.	

Since this story has such a wide array of emotions, it would be a good one to have the children make faces that express the feelings of the people in the story. As you pause while telling the story, make the appropriate expressions and encourage the children to join you.

Paul was a man who didn't like Christians. He was <u>mean</u> . . . and <u>angry</u> at them . . . because he didn't think they were following God!

The Christians were <u>scared</u> of Paul because he put them in jail and wanted to kill them!

One day, Paul was walking along the road toward a city called Damascus when he saw a bright light shine all around him. Paul was <u>totally surprised</u>! . . .

Jesus talked to him and told him to stop hurting the church by attacking Christians. And I think Paul was a little <u>scared</u>! . . . then, when Jesus was done talking to him, Paul couldn't see and he was <u>surprised</u>! . . .

Meanwhile, God told Ananias to go and meet Paul. And Ananias was <u>scared</u> . . . because he knew that Paul attacked Christians, but God told him it would be OK. So then, Ananias <u>felt happy</u> . . . that God had chosen him.

He met Paul and healed him through the power of Jesus. And then, Paul was <u>happy</u> . . . and Ananias was <u>happy</u> . . . that now Paul was a believer!

Paul was baptized and then started to tell people about meeting Jesus on the road to Damascus. And when the people heard him they were <u>surprised</u> . . . because Paul used to attack Christians! But when they found out Paul had really become a believer, the other believers were <u>very, very happy</u> ! . . .

The end.

Summary

Long ago as the church was beginning to grow
Many people didn't like it and wanted to slow
Down the growth of the church, for they didn't understand
That the church was how God spread his love through the land!

One of those people was a fellow named Paul,
And he didn't like Christians, not a bit, not at all.
So he put them in jail and he wanted them dead!
But one day Jesus came in a light and he said,
        "Stop hurting my people and help me instead!"

And the day that Paul saw that mighty white light
Was the day that his soul became shiny and bright!
'Cause he trusted in Jesus, and he made a fresh start
On the day Jesus came to live in his heart!

Chapter 25

Peter Raises Tabitha Back to Life

BASED ON: Acts 9:36-43

BIG IDEA: Through God's power, Peter raised Tabitha, a generous and faithful woman, back to life.

BACKGROUND: Tabitha, a kindhearted woman who was generous to the poor, lived in Joppa. After she died, the disciples showed amazing faith by calling Peter to her home. After praying for her, Peter raised Tabitha from the dead and many people from that area believed in the Lord.

KEY VERSE: "He took her by the hand and helped her to her feet. Then he called the believers and the widows and presented her to them alive. This became known all over Joppa, and many people believed in the Lord" (Acts 9:41, 42).

Once again in this story, God demonstrates his power over death. So once again be sensitive when teaching on the topic of death. Be careful not to downplay it or to dramatize it too much.

Sometimes you can use one simple prop to help you tell a story. Listed below are suggestions for using a scarf to help retell the entire story of Tabitha.

WHAT TO SAY:	SUGGESTED ACTION:
Long ago there was a woman named Tabitha.	Wrap the scarf around your head and neck like women in India or the middle east.
She liked to sew.	Hold the scarf on your lap and pretend to sew it.
She would make clothes for poor people and then give them away for free!	Hold out the scarf as if you are giving it away.
One day, Tabitha became very sick.	Hold the scarf up to your mouth to cover your cough.
She wasn't feeling good at all.	Wipe your brow with the scarf.
Finally, her friends tucked her in bed . . .	Pull the scarf up to your chin.
And soon, poor Tabitha died. Her friends were very sad.	Hold the scarf up to your eyes and dab your tears away.
They called for Peter who came right away.	Wrap the scarf around your neck.
When he arrived, he saw all of Tabitha's friends crying,	Use the scarf to wipe away your tears.
And looking at all the wonderful things Tabitha had made while she was still alive.	Hold up the scarf and admire it.
Peter sent all the other people out of the room and then he leaned over Tabitha's body.	Smooth out the scarf on the ground, as if it were a blanket.
He prayed and then he said to her, "Tabitha get up!" and she did!	Lift up the scarf and wrap it around your head and neck like women in India or the middle east.

He called everyone back in and the women were so happy!	Take off the scarf and wave it in the air to celebrate.
And everyone in the city	Swirl it around to signify how the news spread.
Heard the wonderful story of how God had brought Tabitha	Wrap the scarf around your head and neck like women in India or the middle east.
Back to life through Peter's prayer!	Hold the scarf up in both hands, grasping the ends of it. Lift it high in thanks to the Lord!
The end.	

If you wish, you could use the following ideas instead of the prop-story above, or use the creative drama ideas below to review the story with your children.

Once, long ago, there was a woman named Tabitha. She lived in a town called Joppa and she would make clothes. Sew your clothes, kids . . . Don't poke your finger with a needle! . . .

And she would give the clothes away to poor people. OK, hand out your clothes. Give them away to someone—not the clothes you're wearing, the clothes you're sewing! . . . Oh, my goodness!

But one day, Tabitha became sick. Show me how you look when you're sick . . . Oh, no, look at all these sick kids! . . . She was so sick she had to lie down . . . And then—now don't get scared, kids—but that nice woman died. OK, stand up, because now you get to act like the other people in the story and not like dead Tabitha.

Now, Tabitha's friends were very sad that she died. Do you think they were crying? . . . Show me what they sounded like . . . Good. That's right!

And they sent for Peter who hurried to meet with them. Show me how fast he ran . . . When Peter walked up to the house, he heard all those women crying . . . and he saw them holding up the clothes Tabitha had made while she was still alive. Hold up some of the clothes, kids . . . Don't forget to cry . . . Good. Hold the clothes . . . Cry . . . Clothes . . . Cry . . . Clothes . . . Cry . . . Good!

So, Peter walked over to Tabitha. OK, let's walk over to her . . . He told all the other women to leave for a minute. Then, he knelt down . . . and he prayed. Fold your hands kids and pretend to pray like Peter did! . . .

Peter asked God to bring Tabitha back to life. And then he turned to her and said, "Tabitha get up!" Let's say that with Peter, "TABITHA, GET UP!" . . . Then, Peter took her by the hand and helped her to her feet! . . .

And when everyone saw that she was alive again, they were amazed! Show me how surprised they were! . . . And I'd say they all thanked God too. Let's say, "Thank you, God! You sure are strong!" Ready? "THANK YOU, GOD! YOU SURE ARE STRONG!"

And lots of people heard and believed because God had brought Tabitha back to life again!

The end!

Summary

Tabitha was kind,
And Tabitha was good.
She made clothes for the poor,
And she helped them when she could

But Tabitha got sick one day.
She got so sick she died.
And all the friends of Tabitha
Just cried and cried and cried.

They sent for Peter and he came
To see what he could do.
And he went to see the body
Of the woman that they knew.

He took her hand and then he prayed
That God would help her rise
And suddenly dead Tabitha,
She opened up her eyes!

Tabitha sat up and then
She got up out of bed!
The woman was alive again—
She was no longer dead!

People told their friends and then
They told the folks they knew.
And soon all those who lived nearby
Knew what the Lord can do!

Chapter 26

An Angel Frees Peter from Prison

BASED ON: Acts 12:1-19

BIG IDEA: God answered the prayers of the believers and set Peter free from prison. God still answers the prayers of believers today.

BACKGROUND: As the early church grew, persecution became more and more intense. King Herod arrested Peter, planning to put him to death as he had done to James, the brother of John. When the believers prayed for Peter, neither he nor they could believe how quickly (or how miraculously) God answered their prayers.

KEY VERSE: "Peter followed him out of the prison, but he had no idea that what the angel was doing was really happening; he thought he was seeing a vision" (Acts 12:9).

When King Herod saw how much the murder of the apostle James pleased the Jews, he intended to put Peter to death as well. If you think this is vital to the flow of the story you could include it, but I don't think it's essential information for young children. Many parents are uncomfortable about having their children hear too much about death, dying, or murder.

For the following story, invite the children to sing each refrain with you to the tune of "Mary Had a Little Lamb." As you sing the refrains, have the children join with you and do the suggested actions.

Practice the story a couple of times before class to make sure you're familiar with the refrains and the actions.

WHAT TO SAY:	SUGGESTED REFRAIN:	SUGGESTED ACTIONS:
The king arrested Peter and told sixteen guards to make sure he didn't escape from jail.	This is how we guard the man. Guard the man. Guard the man. This is how we guard the man, The king told us to guard. *(Repeat)*	Flex muscles or draw your sword each time your say "guard our man."
So, Peter was in jail, chained up between two guards. And suddenly an angel appeared and woke Peter up!	This is how we wake from sleep. Wake from sleep. Wake from sleep. This is how we wake from sleep, [When an] angel wakes us up. *(Repeat)*	Yawn and stretch your arms.
The angel told him to put on his clothes and sandals and coat.	This is how we put on clothes. Put on clothes. Put on clothes. This is how we put on clothes, [In the] middle of a prison cell! *(Repeat)*	Put on your clothes!

They walked right past the other guards! But Peter thought he was dreaming! He had no idea it was really happening!	This is how we leave the jail. Leave the jail. Leave the jail. This is how we leave the jail, [While we] think we're still asleep. *(Repeat)*	Walk in place.
They came to the metal door and it opened up all by itself! They walked down the street and then the angel disappeared.	This is how we get surprised! Get surprised! Get surprised! This is how we get surprised! When an angel disappears! *(Repeat)*	Show how surprised you are!
Well then, Peter knew God had sent an angel to free him from jail. So he went to the place where his friends were staying. And he knocked on the door.	This is how we knock real hard. Knock real hard. Knock real hard. This is how we knock real hard, Until they open up! *(Repeat)*	Knock on an imaginary door in front of you.
A girl named Rhoda came to the door, but when she heard Peter's voice she was so excited that she ran to get everyone else, but forgot to open the door! So Peter had to keep on knocking at the door!	This is how we knock even harder! Knock even harder! Knock even harder! This is how we knock even harder, Until they open up! *(Repeat)*	Knock even harder!
Finally, all the people came and found Peter at the door! They let him in and they were very happy God had answered their prayer and set Peter free from jail!	This is how we celebrate! Celebrate! Celebrate This is how we celebrate That God has answered prayer! *(Repeat)*	Dance around!
The end.		

Consider telling this story in two different locations! For example, get two classes together and begin the story in one classroom.

> **Kids, let's all pretend that we are Peter in that prison cell. OK, everyone lie down . . . and let's pretend we're asleep . . . I wonder if anyone snores? . . . Then, an angel appeared! I'll be the angel!**
>
> **Get up . . . put on your coat and sandals . . . Hurry! Let's go! . . .**
>
> *(Lead the children to the door, and then have the other teacher open it from the hallway side and then scurry to the next classroom.)*
>
> **Wow! Look! The door opened up by itself . . . OK, let's go out into the street . . .** *(Lead the children out into the hallway).*

Then, when the angel leads Peter out into the night and down the street, walk down the hallway, and knock on the other classroom door. Say, **"Now I know the angel in the story disappeared before Peter came to his friend's house, but I'll stick around for now. Just pretend I'm invisible."**

Have a teacher from behind the door ask really loudly, "Who's there?" and then have the kids reply, **"IT'S PETER! IT'S PETER! LET ME COME IN!"**

Then, have the teacher behind the door say, "Peter! Oh, my!" and wait. Knock some more and say, **"IT'S PETER! IT'S PETER! LET ME COME IN!"**

Then, from behind the door, have the other teacher yell, "It's Peter! He's at the door! Really, it's him! What do you mean, it's his angel? It's Peter I know; I heard his voice. No, I'm not crazy, come and see for yourself!"

Knock some more. Call some more, **"IT'S PETER! IT'S PETER! LET ME COME IN!"**

Finally, after a bunch more knocking, have the other teacher open the door and say, "Peter! I can hardly believe it's you!" Then enter the classroom and pray for Christians who have been imprisoned in different places in the world for their faith.

Summary

Peter was in jail when a light, it started gleamin'.
(Now he thought he was asleep and that he was only dreamin';)
But an angel came up to him and awoke him with a whackin'!
And Pete was free from all his chains because they were a-crackin'!

And then the angel opened up his mouth and started talkin'
Tellin' Peter to get dressed and then they went a-walkin'.
They passed the guards who might've given him a real bruisin',
(But all the guards just stood there 'cause I guess they were still snoozin'.)

The door outside, it opened wide; the hinges were a-squeakin'.
And out into the night they walked with neither of 'em speakin'.
For Peter still thought he was in a dream and not awakened.
But when the angel disappeared, he knew he'd been mistaken!

He went to find the Christians who were gathered up a-prayin'.
(He knew the place because he knew where everyone was stayin'.)
Then Peter stood outside the door and he continued knockin'
Until they came and answered it, and it was really shockin'!

"It's you!" they said. "It's really you! We thought you were imprisoned!"
"God let me out," he said. "Though I believed it was envisioned!"
They'd prayed for Pete and hoped that God would send some help to aide him;
And God had answered all their prayers, even as they prayed 'em!

Chapter 27

Lydia Becomes a Believer

BASED ON: Acts 16:6-15

BIG IDEA: God directed Paul, Timothy, and Silas to preach in northern Greece. God's kingdom grew as Lydia, the first convert from the continent of Europe, trusted in Christ.

BACKGROUND: Paul and his companions were traveling around sharing the Word of God. As they went, the Holy Spirit directed them toward some regions, and away from others. They were responsive and went where God led them.

KEY VERSE: "One of those listening was a woman named Lydia, a dealer in purple cloth from the city of Thyatira, who was a worshiper of God. The Lord opened her heart to respond to Paul's message" (Acts 16:14).

Even though Lydia worshiped God, she didn't know Christ. Luke records that it was the Lord who opened up Lydia's heart to respond to Paul's message. To be converted from *a religious belief in God* to *a personal belief in Christ* (in order to receive salvation) only occurs through God's grace and by the work of the Holy Spirit in our hearts.

Since Lydia was a seller of dyes and expensive clothes, consider wearing a tie-dye shirt to class today, or (if you're gifted and brave) do some tie-dyeing as a class!

Hey, everyone! My name is Silas! You might not have heard of me before, but I'm good friends with a man named Paul. We teach the Bible together and try to always go where God wants us to go.

So when we were in one place and found out God wanted us to go somewhere else, what do you think we did? Did we stay where we were or go somewhere else? . . . That's right! We went where he showed us because WE WANTED TO DO WHAT GOD TOLD US TO DO!

So one day Paul had a dream and in the dream, he saw a man inviting us to come to his country to share the good news about Jesus!

So, kids, what do you think we did? Did we stay where we were? . . . That's right! We went where God showed us because WE WANTED TO DO WHAT GOD TOLD US TO DO! We figured God was telling us where he wanted us to go next, so we got on a ship and headed to that man's country.

When we go there, we thought we'd find people praying by the river. So did we stay in the city, or did we go out by the river? . . . That's right! We went out by the river. And do you know why? . . . WE WANTED TO DO WHAT GOD TOLD US TO DO!

Well, when we got there, a woman named Lydia was there. She was rich and sold purple clothes. So, we told her about Jesus. And do you know why we did that? . . . WE WANTED TO DO WHAT GOD TOLD US TO DO!

She trusted in Jesus and we baptized her right there in the river! Then, she invited us into her house. "If you consider me a believer," she said, "come and stay at my house!" So, we went to her house. And do you know why we went to her house? . . . WE WANTED TO DO WHAT GOD TOLD US TO DO!

That's right! And God's Word spread through the land as she told her friends and family about Jesus. And we were happy we'd gone to her country. Then we went somewhere else to tell more people about Jesus. And do you know why we went somewhere else? . . . WE WANTED TO DO WHAT GOD TOLD US TO DO!

The end!

(With rhythm)
Paul and Silas told lots of folks about God, *(Turn and talk to each other)*
Folks about God,
Folks about God.
Paul and Silas told lots of folks about God.
When they talked about the Lord! *(Point up to Heaven)*

Sometimes Paul would have a little dream about God, *(Lay your head on your hands)*
Dream about God,
Dream about God.
Sometimes Paul would have a little dream about God,
And he'd tell Paul where to go! *(Point off to the side!)*

One day he had a dream of a man far away, *(Point off to the other side)*
A man far away,
A man far away.
One day he had a dream of a man far away
Who was calling for him to come! *(Cup your hand around your mouth)*

So, Paul and Silas hopped on a boat and sailed, *(Make your hands into sailboats)*
A boat and sailed,
A boat and sailed.
So Paul and Silas hopped on a boat and sailed,
To the place where Paul had dreamed! *(Point to where the man is)*

They went to a place out by the river, *(Walk in place)*
[Out] by the river,
[Out] by the river.
They went to a place out by the river
Where some women went to pray! *(Fold hands)*

They told all those women about the Lord, *(Point up to Heaven!)*
About the Lord,
About the Lord.
They told all those women about the Lord,
And Lydia believed! *(Hands over your heart)*

The Word of God spread all around the land, *(Spread your arms)*
Around the land,
Around the land.
The Word of God spread all around the land,
As they talked about the Lord! *(Point up to Heaven)*

Summary

Paul and Silas spread the Word
And went wherever God led.
And when they listened to God and heard
They'd do whatever he said.

So in a dream, Paul saw a man
From a country far away.
The man wanted them to come to his land
And to preach the word and pray!

So Paul and Silas left in a boat
And went to the place in the dream.
On the day of rest they left the town,
And went out by a stream.

A woman named Lydia and some of her friends
Would meet by the river to pray.
And when she heard Paul talk about God
Lydia trusted in Jesus that day!

Chapter 28

Paul and Silas Leave Prison

BASED ON: Acts 16:16-36

BIG IDEA: God miraculously delivered Paul and Silas from prison and converted the jailer and his family.

BACKGROUND: Paul and Silas, two missionaries in the early Christian church, became unpopular with the slave owners of a girl whom they set free from a demon. As a result, the slave owners incited the citizens of the town to turn on Paul and Silas and the guards were called in.

      After they were beaten and imprisoned, God orchestrated a way for them to be released from prison and to witness to the jail's warden and his family.

KEY VERSE: "The jailer called for lights, rushed in and fell trembling before Paul and Silas. He then brought them out and asked, 'Sirs, what must I do to be saved?'

      They replied, 'Believe in the Lord Jesus, and you will be saved—you and your household'" (Acts 16:29-31).

This story really has two parts to it—the slave girl who was following Paul and Silas, and the earthquake that shook open the jail. However, the two parts go together. The girl was telling everyone, "These men are servants of the Most High God, who are telling you the way to be saved" (Acts 16:17). And then when the guard was frightened that the prisoners were going to escape, he immediately asked Paul and Silas how he could be saved.

If questions come up about the girl who had the spirit that allowed her to tell the future, you can explain to your children that there are angels who turned bad a long time ago called demons, and sometimes they come into people and make those people do things they couldn't do on their own. Angels can see and explain things we can't see.

But God wants us to be filled up with him and not anything bad like demons. That's why Jesus and his friends made demons go away from people.

Since this story might not be as familiar to your students, tell the story without lots of creative dramatics first, before including too many interactive storytelling ideas. This will help assure that the children understand what's going on in the story. However, you could still invite the children to say the refrain with you!

    Paul and his friend Silas were telling people about God. One day, a girl came running up behind them and said:

    (say with rhythm) **These men are from God!**
    These men are from God!
    [And] they'll tell you how you can be saved! *(repeat)*

    Well, normally they would have liked that, but this girl had a demon inside her that helped her tell the future! Some people made lots of money by having her tell what would happen. So Paul and Silas didn't really want her running around saying,
    These men are from God!
    These men are from God!
    [And] they'll tell you how you can be saved! *(repeat)*

    So Paul told the demon to go away, and it did! Well, when that happened, the other people couldn't make money by having the girl tell the future, so they were mad!
    They told the guards to beat up Paul and Silas and put them in jail! And the guard in charge did! He was the jailer. But he remembered what the girl had said . . .

These men are from God!
These men are from God!
[And] they'll tell you how you can be saved! *(repeat)*

That night, when Paul and Silas were in jail there was a big earthquake! The doors flew open and the chains fell away! Who do you think sent that earthquake? . . . That's right, God did!

Well, the jailer was scared all the prisoners would run away from jail, but Paul told him nobody would leave.

Then, the jailer knew God was in charge. He asked Paul and Silas how he could be saved because he remembered the girl had said . . .

These men are from God!
These men are from God!
[And] they'll tell you how you can be saved! *(repeat)*

"Believe in Jesus," they told the jailer. And when they said it, he did it! Then he gave Paul and Silas some food and he bandaged their sores.

So that night, that man and his family became believers and Paul and Silas got to leave the jail the next morning!

God had used the bad events to help save the jailer and his whole family!

The end.

After telling the story to the children, use the following activity to review the scenes and emotions from the story.

If desired, use a real camera to take pictures of the children during the story. If you use a digital camera, you could download the pictures onto a computer to review the story, or post them on a website for your class and let parents know the link so that they can click on it and have their children review the story for them!

OK, I'm going to pretend that I am taking pictures of the different parts of this Bible story and you get to form the pictures that I'm going to take!

First of all, Paul and Silas were upset by the girl who kept following them. Show me how upset they were that she was bugging them, then freeze when I say, "Click!" Ready? 3-2-1 Go! . . . And click! . . . Wow! Great! *(Pretend to take their picture)* . . . All right, you can relax. Stand normal again.

Then, Paul made the demon go away and the girl was free from it forever! She was probably very happy! Show me how she looked, 3-2-1 Go! . . . And click! . . . And, back to normal . . .

But the slave owners were really mad that she couldn't tell the future anymore! Show me how mad they were! 3-2-1 Go! . . . And click! . . . And back to normal . . .

They told the guards that Paul and his friend Silas were breaking the laws! So the guards arrested Paul and Silas and hit them very hard! Show me what those big strong guards looked like when they were going to hit Paul and Silas! 3-2-1 Go! . . . And click! . . . And, back to normal . . .

But Paul and Silas weren't scared. They knew God would take care of them. So they were praising God and singing songs to him even though they were in jail! Ready? 3-2-1 Go! . . . And click! . . . And, back to normal . . .

At about midnight, there was a big earthquake and the doors of the prison flew open and the chains on all the prisoners fell off! Everyone was very surprised! I wonder if anyone fell down during the earthquake? Show me what they looked like during that earthquake! 3-2-1 Go! . . . And click! . . . And, back to normal . . .

Then the jailer thought the prisoners would get away, and he was scared! Ready to look scared? 3-2-1 Go! . . . And click! . . . And, back to normal . . .

But Paul told him no one was leaving. Then the jailer ran in and fell down on his knees and begged Paul and Silas to tell him how he could be saved. Ready to show me that jailer? 3-2-1 Go! . . . And click! . . . And, back to normal . . .

"Believe in Jesus," they told him. "And you will be saved!" That night he believed in Jesus, and then he was full of joy because he had become a Christian. Show me how happy that jailer was! 3-2-1 Go! . . . And click! . . . And, back to normal . . .

That night, his whole family believed in Jesus, and he took care of Paul and Silas. And the next day he let Paul and Silas go from jail. Let's see how happy they were when they were leaving that jail. 3-2-1 Go! . . . And click! . . . And, back to normal . . .

Great job! The end!

Summary

Paul and Silas were put in jail,
But hadn't done anything wrong!
They prayed all night to Jesus Christ
And then they sang a song.

Then suddenly, the jail shook,
And the chains began to break!
And then the doors flew open wide
And the earth began to shake!

The jailer there thought everyone
Would leave and run away!
But Paul just told him,
          "We won't go! Don't worry! We will stay!"

The jailer was so very scared
And a little bit amazed!
He asked if Paul and Silas
Could explain how to be saved.

"Believe in Jesus," they told the man,
And he did just what they said.
And then he woke his family up
And got them out of bed.
And all of them were baptized
Before the dawn arrived.
          (No, the earthquake hadn't hurt them,
          And everyone survived!)

He gave some food to Paul and Silas
And bandaged up their sores.
And then he made sure they were free
To leave the prison doors!

Chapter 29

Paul Faces the Angry Crowds

BASED ON: Acts 21:27–Acts 23

BIG IDEA: God used Paul to spread the good news of the gospel throughout the ancient world, despite the persecution of the Jewish religious leaders.

BACKGROUND: When Jesus first spoke to Paul he was still named Saul and was on his way to send believers to imprisonment or death (see story 24, "Paul Meets Jesus"). God told a man named Ananias to go and meet with Saul, but he was afraid because he'd heard of Saul. At that time, God told Ananias, "Go! This man is my chosen instrument to carry my name before the Gentiles and their kings and before the people of Israel. I will show him how much he must suffer for my name" (Acts 9:15, 16).

In these last chapters of Acts, much of that prophecy is fulfilled as Paul arrives in Jerusalem and is arrested, but also has the chance to proclaim Christ both in the city and to the religious leaders.

KEY VERSE: "The following night the Lord stood near Paul and said, 'Take courage! As you have testified about me in Jerusalem, so you must also testify in Rome'" (Acts 23:11).

Paul faced many hardships and difficulties as a result of his commitment to the Lord and his ministry of preaching to those who had never heard the gospel. (He listed some of the difficulties he faced in 2 Corinthians 11:23-29 in case you'd like to read the full list). Being a Christian doesn't mean that all of life will be easy, but it does mean that all of life (including our suffering) will have a purpose.

Paul came to the city of Jerusalem and began to tell the people all about Jesus. *(Point to various children)* **Jesus loves you, and you, and you, and you, and you, and you, and you!**

As he spoke, some of the people didn't like it and wanted to get rid of him so they started to shout,
(with rhythm) **"MEN OF ISRAEL HELP US,**
THIS FELLOW BREAKS OUR LAWS!
HE TEACHES PEOPLE EVERYWHERE
TO COME AND BREAK OUR LAWS!"
Let's say that . . .

Soon people were running over to see what was going on. People came from all over the city when they heard those men shouting,
"MEN OF ISRAEL HELP US,
THIS FELLOW BREAKS OUR LAWS!
HE TEACHES PEOPLE EVERYWHERE
TO COME AND BREAK OUR LAWS!"

So of course, the people thought Paul was being bad! But was Paul being bad? . . . No he wasn't! He was just telling people that God loved them—*(point to different children)* **Jesus loves you, and you, and you, and you, and you, and you, and you!**

Those men grabbed Paul and dragged him away from the worship place and tried to kill him!

Then, the soldiers heard all the noise and all those people shouting,
"MEN OF ISRAEL HELP US,
THIS FELLOW BREAKS OUR LAWS!
HE TEACHES PEOPLE EVERYWHERE
TO COME AND BREAK OUR LAWS!"

So then the soldiers came running too! And when the people who were hurting Paul saw the soldiers, they stopped beating him up.

The soldiers arrested Paul and started to take him away as all those people kept right on shouting,
"MEN OF ISRAEL HELP US,
THIS FELLOW BREAKS OUR LAWS!
HE TEACHES PEOPLE EVERYWHERE
TO COME AND BREAK OUR LAWS!"

Paul asked the soldier in charge if he could talk to the people. And when they finally quieted down, Paul told the people about the day he met Jesus. They listened until he said God wanted him to tell people all over about Jesus—*(point to different children)* **Jesus loves you, and you, and you, and you, and you, and you, and you!**

Some of the Jewish men didn't like that idea! They thought they should keep God's Word to themselves! So the crowd went crazy! They threw dirt in the air and tossed their jackets to the ground! They wanted the soldiers to kill Paul!

(Loudly and crazily!)
"MEN OF ISRAEL HELP US,
THIS FELLOW BREAKS OUR LAWS!
HE TEACHES PEOPLE EVERYWHERE
TO COME AND BREAK OUR LAWS!"

But instead, the soldiers took Paul away and he was able to tell the story of Jesus to even more people! And finally, God told Paul, **"Don't worry. Don't be scared. You will get to tell people far away in the city of Rome about me."**

So Paul was happy, even though he was in jail. He knew he was doing God's work. And he got to tell people about Jesus—*(pointing again)* **Jesus loves you, and you, and you, and you, and you, and you, and you!**

The end.

Another way of approaching this story would be to explore volume and sound effects as the crowd yells, getting louder and louder, and then is interrupted by the soldiers, and then gets loud again, and then Paul quiets them down, and then they get excited again. When you notice episodes like this, it offers you the chance to make fun loud and soft sound effects for a story!

Summary

Paul was not fearful.
Paul was so brave.
He told everybody
That Jesus can save.
He told all the soldiers
He told all the crowds
He told all the people
      All over the town!

But some didn't like it.
They wanted Paul gone!
They plotted to kill him
From dusk until dawn!
No, they didn't like Paul
And they hated his views.
And they didn't want Paul
      To share the good news.

So they had him arrested!
They sent him to jail!
They wanted Paul's mission
To finally fail!
But he didn't stop preaching,
Paul did what God said.
And he helped all the churches
      To grow and to spread!

Chapter 30

The Great Shipwreck

BASED ON: Acts 27, 28

BIG IDEA: On the way to Rome, the ship on which Paul and Luke were sailing was caught in hurricane-force winds. After the shipwreck, many sailors and islanders heard about and witnessed God's power and grace.

BACKGROUND: Paul had been imprisoned. As a Roman citizen, he had the right to appeal his case to Caesar. When he did that, a Roman soldier named Julius was put in charge of assuring that Paul arrived safely in Rome.

Immediately after starting their trip, they ran into bad weather. The story of their shipwreck and the survival of all 276 sailors and passengers is a testament to God's grace and provision.

KEY VERSE: "Last night an angel of the God whose I am and whom I serve stood beside me and said, 'Do not be afraid, Paul. You must stand trial before Caesar; and God has graciously given you the lives of all who sail with you'" (Acts 27:23, 24).

This story might seem a little long and confusing since it stretches over two chapters of the Bible, and includes quite a number of place names and towns. However, by simply focusing on the action, it makes a great story to tell younger children.

Invite the students on an imaginary journey to pretend they're getting ready for the storm. (You may wish to have a spray bottle of water, a fan, and a helper available before beginning this story!)

> **Today's story will be lots of fun. Let's get ready to hear it . . .**
> **Oh, no! It looks like it's gonna rain outside! Quick, everyone, shut the door**! *(As you go through these activities, act them out)* . . . **Close the windows . . . Grab a warm blanket and wrap yourself up in it . . . Can you feel the wind blow?** *(If desired, have a helper turn on a fan and aim it at the students)* . . . **Make the sound of a mighty wind! . . . Oh, no! Here comes the lightning! . . .** *(Have a helper flicker the lights in your room).*
> **And the thunder! . . .** *(Have your helper make loud, scary sounds)* . . . **Is everyone safe from the storm? Good! . . . Here comes the water! Catch some raindrops on your tongues . . .** *(If desired, have your helper spray water at the children)* . . . **OK! Now, let's find out what's going on in this story . . . Let's see if our boat can stand up to this storm! . . .** [7]

It would be fun to have a fan you can direct at the students and turn up from low to high during different parts of the story!

> (PART 1)
> **Some men were taking Paul to Rome on a great big sailing ship! OK, everyone, climb aboard . . . But while they were on the sea, a big wind blew up! Oh, oh! It's really windy here!** *(rock back and forth)* . . . **Don't fall over in the wind! . . .**
> **They tried to stop the boat, but the wind was so strong it blew the ship out to sea! . . . So, they pulled up the lifeboat! Pull it up! . . . Pull it up . . . Pull it up! . . .**
> **Then they tied ropes around the boat to keep it from falling apart! OK, let's tie ropes around the boat . . .**

Then they lowered the anchor to try and slow down the boat! Lower your anchors, kids! But don't drop the anchor on your foot! . . .

When the wind wouldn't stop, the people started throwing stuff overboard to make the boat lighter! . . . Big things . . . and small things . . . big things . . . and small things . . .

(PART 2)

The clouds covered the sun and it was really dark all day long! Close your eyes! It's so dark . . .

Then, Paul told the people on the ship that an angel had appeared before him! Show me your great big angel wings! . . . Wow!

The angel told him that they would all be OK, but that the ship was going to sink! *(make your hand sink like a boat).*

Then the ship was about to get smashed, so they tried to stop it from hitting the rocks by tossing out three anchors! Ready? Anchor number one! . . . Anchor number two! . . . Anchor number three! . . . Don't let it fall on your foot! . . . Ow! . . .

Some men were trying to lower the lifeboat to escape! Quick, cut the ropes to let the lifeboat float away . . . Whew . . . If they would have gotten away, Paul said everyone might not be OK!

(PART 3)

Oh, my! We've been so scared and so busy that we haven't eaten any food! . . . Everyone on the ship is so hungry! . . . Oh, good! Paul is thanking God for some food and breaking the bread and handing it out! Who wants some food?! *(toss out imaginary food to all the kids)* . . . Who else? . . . OK, everybody eat up your food! . . . Is it yummy? . . . Ah, now I feel much better!

But our ship is still getting blown around! Let's throw some more stuff overboard! Big things . . . and small things . . . big things . . . and small things . . .

There's a beach up ahead! Let's see if we can get the ship to go up on the beach! Cut the ropes that are holding the anchors . . . Don't let the rope get tangled around your foot and pull you into the water . . . Oh, brother!

(PART 4)

Then the ship started breaking up in the waves! We have to get off before it breaks into pieces! . . . Everybody jump overboard! . . . And swim! . . . Swim! . . . Swim! . . . If you don't know how to swim, grab a piece of floating wood and hold onto that! . . . Hurry! Don't sink under the water! . . .

OK, float up over the big waves . . . Swim! Swim! Swim! . . . And float . . . And swim! . . . Float . . . Swim! . . .

Whew! We made it to shore! OK, everybody, climb up out of the water and have a seat! . . . Let's relax! The people on this island are nice and will help take care of us!

Yes, God promised Paul the men would be safe and then, God protected them in the big storm. God was protecting Paul on his trip to Rome where Paul would be able to tell all the people about Jesus!

The end.

Have fun retelling this story with a big tub of water, little green army men, a small boat, a fan, and a squirt gun. Spray water on the men, tip the boat over, aim the fan at the water, and use your hands swirling through the water to make big waves. Create your own hurricane. Be aware that the children will want to join you, so you may want to only do this on a special day when all the kids can get a little wet!

Summary

The sea was very stormy and the waves were very rough!
And the sailors were all terrified, though all of them were tough!
"We will not die," Paul told the men. "And here is how I know:
      An angel from the Lord came in a dream and told me so!"

The waves were getting bigger. The wind was blowing more.
It pushed their boat out farther and farther from the shore.
They threw stuff overboard and dropped their anchors in the deep.
And they were very terrified and didn't get much sleep!

At last the boat hit a sandbar that was laying near a beach,
And the captain yelled above the storm to make a little speech.
      "We'll meet on shore! Grab wood to float. Now go swim through the sea!"
And in the end, the men were safe, just like God said they'd be.

Understanding Young Children

Young children present special challenges for the creative storyteller. After all, their little bodies aren't made for sitting still! They wiggle and squirm and run around and look at birds flying past the window and play with their shoelaces and just want to have fun!

In this chapter, you'll learn five characteristics of young minds, and how each characteristic affects how you can more effectively communicate with children.[8]

Abstract vs. Concrete

Young children don't think in abstract terms. They won't easily understand the hidden meanings, metaphors, and symbolism in stories. Usually, the power of parables comes from weaving a spiritual truth into a story that's essentially about something else. The more abstract the parallels, the less young children will grasp their meaning.

For example, when Jesus told a story about a lost sheep, he was using a story about an event from his culture to show the similarities of how we spiritually wander from God, and how God takes the initiative to look for us and rescue us—and then celebrates when we're found.

But for young children, it's a story about a lost sheep. Period. They won't understand all the spiritual parallels.

This doesn't mean you should *never* tell parables to young children, just be aware that you may need to explain the symbolism in as concrete a way as you can: "That shepherd cared for the sheep enough to go and find it and bring it home. God loves us just like that. He loves you and wants to bring you home to heaven."

So, as you craft stories for young children, look for simple, clear, easy-to-understand stories that are concrete rather than abstract.

Sitting Still vs. Paying Attention

One day when my daughter Ariel was four years old I dropped her off at a church's day care program. When I picked her up a few hours later and asked her if she had fun, she shook her head no.

"Why not?" I asked.

"We watched a movie."

"Well that sounds like fun. Why wasn't it fun?"

Then she explained that the teacher had told them that if they moved during the movie, they wouldn't get a snack.

"Well, what was the movie about?" I asked.

"I don't know," Ariel replied. She'd been concentrating so hard on not moving, that she couldn't pay attention to the movie!

Don't mistake sitting still for paying attention. Listening is not the same thing as sitting still. For many young children, sitting motionless is much more work than paying attention. And it's nearly impossible for them to do both at the same time.

Listening, really listening, is tiring. It's not the same as watching TV, because when you listen to a story, you're responsible for creating all of the images of the story in your mind. Remember, children love listening to stories, but sitting still while someone talks to them sounds like a lot of work and not a whole lot of fun. So, focus more time and energy on grabbing and keeping the attention of the children rather than trying to get them to sit still.

Some people claim that young children have a short attention span. "Children can only pay attention for one minute for each year they are old," someone told me once. I struggled with that because, while I understood where this woman was coming from, I'd seen preschool children sit and listen to me telling stories for twenty-five minutes or more at a time.

Then one day, early childhood expert and author Mary Manz Simon asked me, "Do you think children have a short attention span?"

As I fumbled for an answer she said, "If they did, Steven, how could they play in the bathtub for half an hour at a time?"

Yes! I'd finally found someone who shared my perspective!

I think the secret is that children don't have a short attention span; they have a large distraction span! If they're interested, engaged, and involved they'll be able to pay close attention for quite a while. But they can also be easily distracted. So be sure to remove distractions before starting your story. Make sure there isn't a door behind you that someone might walk through, or other teachers preparing snacks in view of the children, or music from another room floating through the walls.

The challenge is to tell stories in a way that your students can understand and relate to, that engages their imaginations, and that actively involves their bodies.

How do we do this? By choosing appropriate material, taking the time to prepare and shape it so that it connects with our students, and then by telling our stories with energy, imagination, enthusiasm, and participation.

One more thing: sometimes it's helpful to give children a mental break in-between stories. Chant a Bible verse with them, do an object lesson, have a short contest, or do a brief skit. Then, after you've given their imaginations a quick break, transition into the next story.

Reading vs. Telling

One night, I finished reading a bedtime story to my oldest daughter (who was two years old at the time) and closed the book.

She snuggled close to me and said, "Daddy, can you tell me a story with your mouth?"

"What do you mean, Honey?" I asked. "I just read you a story!"

And then it hit me.

"Do you want me to tell you a story without the book?"

Her eyes lit up. "Uh-huh!"

I learned an important lesson that day: she didn't want a story from the pages of a book, but from the pages of my heart. She wanted me to tell it with my mouth.

Many educators simply read each lesson or story from their church's Bible curriculum. While there's nothing wrong with studying the ideas found in your curriculum, be aware that the way the story is written in this book (or any other) is not necessarily the "right" way for you to tell it to your students. You're a different storyteller than the author, and your class is unique. It's much more important for you to connect the story to the lives of your students than to "get through the material" in each lesson.

So look for ways to learn and tell the story yourself (from your own mouth and in your own way!) rather than just reading it from the pages of a book.

Explaining Stories vs. Telling Stories

For the most part, children (and adults) will pay attention only as long as they're curious about what's happening. In other words, if you're telling a story and the children know how it will end or how it will get to the end, they begin to lose interest. Children will start thinking about snack time, crafts, or playing on the playground.

So, use your children's natural curiosity to your advantage. Don't tell them what the story will be about. Instead, do all you can to ignite and foster their curiosity!

I've found that the more time I spend preparing my lessons, the less time I end up lecturing, and the more the children end up learning. But the less time I spend preparing my lessons, the more I lecture and the less they learn.

If kids aren't having fun, they probably aren't learning. And if kids are interested and engaged in the lesson, they probably aren't misbehaving.

So spend more time preparing your lessons and thinking through transitions from one activity to another. Look for ways to include more learning activities, attention-getting object lessons, and interactive storytelling in your teaching time.

If things get boring, direct the attention of the students to another activity. Remove distractions and keep the children focused. A good rule of thumb to remember is this: the younger the children you're speaking to, the shorter you'll want to make the stories you're telling. Also, the more you explain a story, the less impact it has. So spend less time and effort explaining what every story is supposed to mean and more effort telling it in an exciting and engaging way in the first place.

Asking Questions vs. Telling Stories

Have you ever heard (or said!) something like this?

"OK, boys and girls, today we're going to learn about Noah and the ark! Noah took lots of animals on the ark. What were some of the animals? That's right, he took horses. Horses live on farms. Has anyone ever been to a farm? What did you see? Were there cows there? Cows give us milk to drink in our cereal. What's your favorite type of cereal? . . ."

I can just picture what happens when the parents pick up their children, "So, Joey, what did you learn at Sunday School today?"

"I don't know. . . . Something about how Noah fed Fruit Loops to the horses on the ark. . . ."

Asking children too many questions while you tell a story can bewilder children, distract them, and lead you into tangents. So, ask fewer questions and don't be afraid to just tell the story.

Sometimes teachers ask all these questions "to get them to pay attention." But a poorly directed question will often distract rather than focus children.

Many educators, when telling the story of "Jonah and The Big Fish," say things like, "Boys and girls, today's story is about a great big fish. Ooh! Who likes to go fishing? Wow!"

Now, the problem with this approach is that, without realizing it, you've just changed the subject. Instead of thinking about Jonah, the children are thinking about a fishing adventure they've been on. And then, a few minutes later when the children want to talk about their fishing trip, the teacher feels like they "aren't paying attention to the story." In truth, they were paying attention, but then got sidetracked by the teacher's question! And besides, Jonah has nothing to do with a fishing trip. No one goes fishing in the story so why bring up a fishing trip in the first place?

Whenever you ask questions, make sure they're not open-ended questions that will get the children thinking about something other than the story you're telling.

If you ask any questions, let each question direct attention to the main point of the story: "Kids, how many of you have ever been afraid of getting in trouble?" (As you ask this, raise your own hand so they know to answer with their hands, not their mouths.) "How many of you have ever said 'No!' when your mommy or daddy asked you to do something? Me, too! Today's story is about a man who lived long ago who said 'No!' to God . . ."

Remember, every question you ask must move the story forward, not cause your children to become distracted from the story.

So, in summary,

• Young children can't sit still for long. They love to move, play and wiggle—it's how they pay attention! So find ways to help them wiggle during the stories and be patient with them if they move around a little during the storytelling time.

• Young children love to play pretend. So, foster and nurture their curiosity, imagination, and sense of wonder.

• Young children would rather hear a story told than explained. So, tell your stories in an exciting way and make your summaries and sermons short, concrete, and to the point.

• Young children can't understand abstract concepts. So, avoid elaborate analogies and metaphors and focus instead on simple stories and illustrations from your children's world.

• Young children are easily distracted. So make sure you've created a storytelling environment that has few (or no!) distracting things to look at, listen to, touch, or do.

20 Ways to Let Young Children Know You Love Them[9]

- **Notice me.** It's easy to look over my head, ignore me, or step around me. Take the time to get down on my level and look me in the eyes. I never want to feel like I'm in the way.

- **When I put my arms up toward you, hug me.** Sometimes I just need to be held, even if it's only for a moment.

- **Tell me the truth, but not all of it at once.** I'm not ready to hear some things yet. Just a little bit at a time. Be patient. And don't worry; I'll believe you even if I don't understand you.

- **Snuggle with me on rainy days.**

- **Be gentle with words.** Sticks and stones may break my bones, but words may bruise my heart.

- **Protect me from the dark places, the bullies, and the monsters of the world.** I can be easily frightened, intimidated, and misled. Sometimes I need you to guard me and stand up for me.

- **Smile at me.** It makes me feel welcomed, loved, and important!

- **Share my excitement when something special happens.** I love to celebrate life! Join me!

- **Forgive me quickly.** I promise I'll do the same for you. And tell me that God isn't angry at me anymore, either.

- **Go ahead and tickle me, but stop when I ask you to.**

- **Let me giggle and fall over laughing sometimes.** And join me when I do! Remember, it's OK to be silly. It doesn't mean you're childish, just childlike.

- **Teach me when it's OK to cry.** Be willing to dry my tears when they come. Comfort me when I'm scared and let me know that I'll be safe whenever I'm with you.

- **Admit your mistakes.** Remember, I'm watching you to learn how a big person should act.

- **Pray with me.** Pray for me. And teach me to pray, too.

- **Spend time with me, even if it's not doing anything special.** I want you to be my friend and I just like being with people who care about me. I'll bet you do, too!

- **Let me wish. And dream. And pretend.** These are great ways to help me to learn that the most important things in life are all invisible.

- **Discipline me when I misbehave.** Sometimes I'll disobey just to see if you notice. Even though I don't like to be punished, I'm glad you care enough to teach me right from wrong.

- **Remember that hugs speak louder than words.**

- **Listen to me, especially when I'm sad.** That's when I really need a friend.

- **Tell me every day how much God loves me.** And show me what that kind of love looks like in the real world.

How to Make Your Stories SOAR!

Now that we've explored some of the characteristics of this age group, let's look at some specific ways you can creatively and effectively tell stories to young children.

Step 1
Study the story

When a pilot taxis down the runway, he knows where he's going to land before he takes off. He begins with his destination in mind. Storytellers do the same thing! We begin with the end in mind. We start by looking at the end of the story first.

The beginning of a story is more than just the first thing that happens in a story. The beginning is the originating action, the one that sets in motion all that will follow. And the end of the story is the resolution. So look closely at the story as a whole. To grasp what a story is really about, ask what's going on, who struggles, what they discover, and how that changes their life or situation.

Sometimes as you study a story, you'll realize that some of the language or content of the story isn't appropriate for young children. Take King David, for example. His adventures were often bloody, brutal, and very graphic. His sins (murder, adultery, and pride) resulted in the deaths of tens of thousands of people! Yet, David is a favorite for curriculum authors of stories for young children. While he's certainly a great hero of the faith, you need to be careful when telling his stories so that you don't frighten, shock, or confuse young children.

Step 2
Look for ways to include participation

I like to keep the acronym SOAR in mind when I'm preparing stories for children ages 3-7. It was the starting point of every chapter in this book and, when you understand the concepts involved, you'll be able to come up with engaging, fun, and interesting ways of telling stories to young children all by yourself.

<u>Sounds</u> OAR

The first thing to look for in a story is **sounds**. What sounds naturally occur in this story? Could the children make sound effects? Maybe animals appear in the story and you can make the animal sounds, or maybe the children can recreate the sound of the storm that Jesus calmed, or the snoring disciples in the Garden of Gethsemane. Search for sounds that you and the children can make to keep everyone engaged in the story.

Here are seven ways to incorporate music, instruments, sound effects, chants, rhythm, and rhymes in your storytelling.

1. Make music with instruments: Use simple instruments such as kazoos, bells, xylophones, rain sticks, wood blocks, drums, maracas, or tambourines to allow children to make music during some (or all) of the story. You can use the instrument yourself, have a small group of children accompany you, or you can give instruments to the whole class!

You may wish to create your own simple rhythm instruments with beans, sticks, cardboard tubes, sand, or shells. Pour beans or sand into a container, seal the opening, and you've got a shaker! You can also use instruments to create background sounds or music for specific sections of your story.

2. Make music with your body: Children can join you by clapping their hands, tapping their feet, snapping their fingers, slapping their knees, or rubbing their hands together! (The younger the children, the tougher it'll be for them to "keep a beat." So be patient!)

3. Make music by singing: Songs often appear in Bible stories. Many times when David was going through a tough time, he wrote a song about it! As you tell those stories, you could sing lines from the Psalms he wrote.

Or make up simple melodies for the refrains of your stories, sing worship songs, or listen to songs that summarize Bible stories. You may wish to sing a popular song or hymn and then tell the story about the person who wrote it, or when and why it was written.

4. Make music with a cheer, chant, or rap: Think of a cheer, chant, or rap that you can use as a refrain for the story. Create a way of telling the whole story, or part of the story, in rhyme!

If you have a large group, you may wish to divide the audience into sections or groups and assign each section a different part or refrain to say or sing.

5. Make music by adding a call and response section: When using "call and response" storytelling, you read or say a section of the story and the audience responds by saying or doing something.

Some Psalms are set up this way. See Psalm 136 for an example of a simple story-song that includes a refrain your children could say or sing!

6. Add mood music: Find instrumental music that reflects the mood of the story. Or, look for CDs with sound effects that a helper can cue during the telling of the story, or search online and download appropriate sound effects. You may even have a talented instrumentalist at your church who can improvise music on a keyboard or guitar as you tell the story!

7. Make your own sound effects: A story rich in sounds is the story of Noah's Ark (Genesis 6-9). You could reenact the sounds of the building process (cutting wood, stacking, painting), the sounds of the animals (roaring, chirping, howling), the sounds of evil people (grunting, screaming, cackling) and the sounds of the storm (raining, blowing, thundering).

Sound effects are easy to add whenever there are animals, specific environments in your stories (such as jungles, night scenes, or crowded markets), or weather-related scenes (such as storms, wind, or thunder). Cue the audience when to participate, when to get louder, and when to be as soft as possible. You can also invite the children to join you by booing or cheering during different sections of a story!

Sounds Objects AR

Next, look for **objects** that appear in the story, or brainstorm ways that you could use simple objects to help you tell the story.

For example, you may wish to use a surprise bag when you tell stories. As you tell the story, pull out objects for the students to see, smell, touch, or taste. They'll pay close attention because they'll wonder what you're going to pull out next!

Here are nine ideas for using simple costumes, props, and objects for telling stories to young children.

1. Wear a silly costume: Keep the costume simple—perhaps just a hat, sunglasses, or a wig. Children love it when adults wear silly clothes or goofy costumes. Having a few simple costume pieces on hand can add lots of fun to the stories you tell.

2. Use a puppet: Consider using finger puppets, hand puppets, or arm puppets. Remember when using a puppet to (1) only open and close its mouth on each syllable (i.e. as you open and close your own mouth), (2) always keep the puppet moving, and (3) have the puppet look at whomever he is talking to. By following these three simple steps, you'll create the illusion that the puppet is alive and it won't matter that you move your lips when you tell the story.

3. Bring out the toys: Use stuffed animals, toys, dolls, army men, and action figures as props.

4. Serve food: Eat foods that are referred to in the story, eaten in the story, or related to the story. Create your own edible object lessons using pretzels, gum drops, marshmallows, raisins, crackers, cheese, apple slices, or peanut butter (warning: some children are seriously allergic to peanuts!).

5. Tell a story with a felt board: Use cut-out felt figures and a colorful background to tell the story. There are many fine felt boards and figures commercially available.

6. Hand out scarves: Use crepe paper, ribbons, streamers, banners, or scarves to represent fire, wind or water. Have children wave them at appropriate times in the story.

7. Blow bubbles: Blow bubbles whenever God or an angel speaks in a story.

8. Sensory Props: By appealing to the senses you'll help the children better remember the stories.
- **Sight**—Turn off the lights, flicker them, or use filters to create different-colored lighting.
- **Touch**—Use squirt guns when telling stories of storms, rain, or floods. Use fingerpaints with younger children. Use a fan to create wind, or a hair dryer to create a hot desert wind!
- **Hearing**—Add music, sound effects, or funny noises to the story.
- **Taste**—Eat food that relates to the story. Something sweet (like honey) can represent manna or God's Word!
- **Smell**—Place candy or oranges in a bag to create a sweet smell. Use stinky garbage to represent sin!

9. Manipulatives: Use anything that can be changed into another shape or form to show the transition of the main character, or to represent different objects that appear throughout the story.
- paper can be cut, crinkled, or folded.
- aluminum foil can be squeezed, flattened, or molded.
- pipe cleaners can be bent, twisted, or curled.
- string can be cut, tied, or designed.

Sounds Objects Actions R

Third, look for **actions** that appear in the story, or for ways to act out what happens in the story. You can use creative dramatics to help introduce the story you wish to tell, dramatize the story as you tell it, or review the story after you've finished telling it.

Whenever you invite the students to join you in movement or creative dramatics, be sure to create an atmosphere in which participation is safe, encouraged, and fun. Invite people to participate but don't force them to. Clearly explain when you want the children to join you, what you want them to do, and when they should stop. You might say, "Whenever I put on my hat you'll start making the sound of the lions in the cave, but when I take it off, you'll stop. Let's practice . . ."

Remember, you can have students use their fingers, gestures, facial expressions, or they can use their whole bodies to act out parts of the story. Consider using sign language, bouncing in place, pretending to walk, waving arms, tapping feet, or using other simple movements. (Be aware that younger children may have a tough time clapping and singing at the same time.) Exaggerated actions are funniest, so let loose and have fun!

Sounds Objects Actions Repetition

Finally, look for **repetition** that naturally occurs within the story. It might be the repetition of a specific phrase (such as, "And God looked at what he'd made and it was good!") or a series of events. For example, when God was calling to Samuel in 1 Samuel 3, repetition occurs as God calls to Samuel, Samuel runs to see what Eli wants (since he thinks the voice is Eli), and Eli sends him back to bed. This process happens three times. You could create a refrain to say each time Samuel runs to Eli, or have the children run back and forth from different sides of the room whenever you come to that part of the story.

Repetition occurs naturally in many types of stories. For example, think of the stories of "The Three Bears," "The Three Little Pigs," or "The Three Billy Goats Gruff." See how the number "3" occurs in each of them? Now, think of Scripture. How many times did Peter deny Jesus? Three. How many times did Jesus ask Peter if he loved him? Three. How many people came up to the Good Samaritan as he lay in the ditch? Three. How many times did Jesus return to the sleeping disciples in the Garden of Gethsemane? Three! See all that repetition?

God knows we remember things best when they're repeated. That's how we're wired to remember them. And that's why God imbedded repetition all throughout his story in the Bible!

Every time you find repetition, you can invite the children to say or act out a part of the story with you.

Step 3
Put it all together

Many people think they're not very creative, but usually they can come up with great ideas if only they would begin by limiting themselves in specific ways. For example, limiting yourself to thinking of specific sounds, objects, actions, or repetitious sections that appear in the story. Once we do that, we discover that we're a lot more creative than we ever thought we were.

I was teaching a creative storytelling seminar in Ohio one time when a first grade teacher came up to me and said, "I wish I were creative like you. I'm just not creative. I can't think of anything to do with my students. Can you come teach my class?"

"Well, what lesson are you teaching?"

She sighed. "The story of Jesus calming the storm. But I'm just not creative like you."

"Well," I said, "first you need to limit yourself. Think of ways to help the story SOAR. Are there any sounds in the story?"

She nodded. "Yes, there's the sound of the storm and the sleeping disciples. We could make the sound of thunder or rain falling on the water or the snoring disciples, but I'm just not creative. I wish I was creative like you."

"Um, are there any objects in the story?"

She took a deep breath. "Well, there's water and a boat and Jesus is laying his head on a pillow. So, we could maybe get a blue blanket and all hold the edges and put something in the middle of it, like a ball or something, and that could be the boat and we could all shake the blanket to make the storm and then hold it still when the water is calmed, but I just can't think of anything."

"OK, what about actions?" I asked, looking at her curiously. "Are there any actions in the story?"

She sighed again. "I suppose we could act out being the raindrops or we could swing our arms to make the waves or we could pretend to be sleeping and then get up as Jesus did. Half the class could be the storm and the other half the disciples. Oh, can't you come teach my class, you're so creative!"

By then I was getting a bit exasperated. She was so full of ideas but she just couldn't see it because she'd been telling herself for so many years how uncreative she was! "What about repetition?" I asked.

"Yes, yes, there's repetition. The rain falling and the disciples trying to wake Jesus and the waves rushing against the boat. I guess we could make up a refrain or something, I just wish I were creative like you."

"I wish I were creative like you!" I said. And only then did it begin to dawn on her that she could come up with creative ideas all on her own.

Once you begin to think in terms of sounds, objects, actions, and repetition, you won't even need a book like this! You'll have more ideas than you could ever need. (But this will be our little secret. Don't tell your friends this until after they've bought a copy for themselves.)

Practice your story, but don't try to memorize it. Feel free to change the story and adapt it (even while you're telling it)! And trust that God will use you to impact young lives when you're faithful in serving him.

Oh, one more thing. You won't always use all of these ideas (sounds, objects, actions, and repetition) for every story. That would be a bit too much. Instead, use each idea judiciously.

Also, remember to let the way you tell the story grow out of your own personality, gifts, and interests. It's more important for you to connect with the students than for you to read the story as it's found in this (or any) book. Feel free to change the story to make better use of your own special God-given gifts and to more appropriately connect with your students. To review, here are the steps to follow when developing the stories you are going to tell:

1. Read the story in context and try to discover what's going on in the background. Look for the big picture. Study the context. Who were the listeners? Why was this story told? Often the context of the story will give you clues about the point of the story or the intended application of the story.

2. Figure out what the story is really about. Don't worry so much about being able to summarize the story in a tidy little topical sentence. Instead, try to let the story move you to the place where God wants you to be. Connect with the story not just in your head, but also in your heart.

Then, look for a natural way to let the audience reach that point too (without your having to explain to them what they're supposed to be feeling). As you retell the story, ask, "Who changes? How is she at the beginning of the story? How is she different at the end of the story?"

3. Look at the structure of the story. Some stories have lots of action; others have lots of dialogue. Ask yourself, "Is this a story that I mainly *hear*, or one that I mainly *see*? How might that affect the way I retell it to my students?"

Some stories have lots of repetition. What about this story? If not, what's the flow of the action? Where does the action occur? Does the setting or scenery change throughout the story? How will the different scenes help you remember the flow of the story?

4. Think about how you're going to retell this story. Are there issues or events that occur in this story that might be inappropriate for the age group you're teaching? How will you handle those?

As you think about how to tell the story, always keep your students in mind. How will your children respond to this story? Are there concepts or words that your students won't understand? If so, what are some similar words you could use that'll help the children better relate to the story?

5. Practice telling yourself about the story. Try to picture it for yourself. Try retelling the story in your own words and describe what you see. How will you describe the scenery or the characters in a way that will help your listeners picture them in their own imaginations? What images, characters, or events in this story move you? How can you weave those emotions into the story?

6. Connect creative storytelling techniques to the story. Look for ways to include sounds, objects, actions, and repetition in retelling the story. Think of ways to make the story memorable, engaging, and interactive. Ask yourself if there are specific storytelling techniques that naturally lend themselves to this story (for example, audience participation, music, silly props, creative dramatics, etc.). Then, weave those into the way that you practice and rehearse the story.

7. Prepare your story with your audience in mind. You've taken the time to better understand your story, to think through the flow of the story, to personally connect with it, and you've looked for creative ways to retell it. Now it's time to practice your story with your students in mind. Pay special attention to the beginning, the ending, and the transitions to and from any audience participation sections.

Avoid the temptation to "polish" the story in a specific way; rather, spend your time really getting to know the story so that you can adapt it to your specific audience and respond to the reaction of the children as you tell the story. As you practice the story, pay attention to how it's going and keep any changes, phrases, or comments that add to the story. Have fun, relax, enjoy yourself, and trust that God will do something exciting as you let yourself be used by him.

Ten Tips for Telling Stories to Young Children

1. Speak With Respect—A strange thing happens to many otherwise normal adults when they start to tell stories to young children. They begin talking in a sappy, sing-songy voice that doesn't sound real or genuine. It makes me think of Barney on helium! Don't talk down to your students. Instead, talk to them in a natural, energetic, and lively way that doesn't belittle them.

2. Choose Appropriate Stories—Some stories in Scripture deal with themes and issues that young children aren't ready to understand or even hear about. Not all parents agree on which subjects their children should be exposed to at a young age. So be honest but not always forthcoming about what information appears in the stories you're teaching young children. Avoid dealing with death, sex, violence, adult themes and adult language in your stories. Leave out graphic details that young kids aren't ready to hear.

3. Start at the End—Before beginning to work on your story, read through the story in the Bible. Look at what comes before and after the story to see the context in which it was told. Take the time to really study and get to the heart of the story. Then, look for the main point of the story and see who it's really about. Avoid stories with too many characters or too much symbolism. Ask yourself, "Will my students really understand this story?" Especially with younger children, ask what changes in wording, content, or order you may need to make to the story.

4. Create Simple Refrains—Look for repetition, simple plots, and simple resolutions. Nail down the main idea and then add a chant, movement, or instrument.

5. Stay Focused on the Story—Rather than asking lots of questions during the story (which can distract the children), stay focused on the action and emotion of the story. As you tell the story, watch your students. Look at their faces to see if they understand and enjoy the story. You can usually tell if you're making a story too long or too frightening by the size of your students' eyes. Keep the stories short, simple, and action-packed.

6. Look for Connections—As you study and prepare your story, look for sounds, objects, actions, and repetition in the story. If you can find ways to connect the story to music, creative dramatics, or movement, you'll be able to easily include audience involvement.

7. Tell the Story Your Own Way—Tell the story in your own words; don't try to remember "the right words." Use natural gestures. Some people "talk with their hands." If that's natural for you, great! If not, don't try to imitate someone else. Do what's most natural for you. Funny faces, funny voices, and silly costumes will work well for this age group!

8. Move Through the Story—Let your body help you tell the story. If a character in your story is large and scary, stand big and lower your voice. If the character is tiny, scrunch up small. As you practice the story, practice your movement, inflection, and gestures.

9. Tell the Story First—This book includes hundreds of helpful ideas and storytelling suggestions for audience participation. However, if your children are unfamiliar with a story, you might wish to tell the story first and then invite them to act out the story so that the children understand what's going on in the story and can remember the sequence of events. Then, after telling the whole story, say, *"OK, everyone! Now, let's have some fun with this story! Let's act it out"*

10. Relax and Enjoy! —Smile and have fun as you tell your stories. Value this time of connection with your students. Tell the story with lots of expression and don't be afraid to get a little silly. Rely on God and let him work through you!

1 (page 6) An earlier version of this story first appeared in *The Creative Storytelling Guide for Children's Ministry* (Standard, 2002) by Steven James. Used by permission.

2 (page 7) This poem first appeared in *Believe It: Bible Basics that Won't Break Your Brain* (Standard, 2003) by Steven James. Used by permission.

3 (page 11) An earlier version of this story first appeared in *The Creative Storytelling Guide for Children's Ministry* (Standard, 2002) by Steven James. Used by permission.

4 (page 33) This poem first appeared in *Believe It: Bible Basics that Won't Break Your Brain* (Standard, 2003) by Steven James. Used by permission.

5 (page 34) An earlier version of this story first appeared in *The Creative Storytelling Guide for Children's Ministry* (Standard, 2002) by Steven James. Used by permission.

6 (page 37) This poem first appeared in *Believe It: Bible Basics that Won't Break Your Brain* (Standard, 2003) by Steven James. Used by permission.

7 (page 97) This introductory activity is based on a story that first appeared in *Sharable Parables: Creative Storytelling Ideas for Ages 3-12* (Standard, 2005) by Steven James. Used by permission.

8 (page 100) Some of the content in the appendices is based on material from *The Creative Storytelling Guide for Children's Ministry* (Standard, 2002), and *Sharable Parables* (Standard, 2005) by Steven James. Used by permission. The information has been adapted and expanded for this book.

9 (page 103) Excerpted from *"Fill 'Em Up"* a Children's Ministry Seminar written by Steven James for the International Network of Children's Ministry. © 2001. All rights reserved. Used by permission.

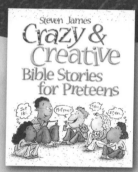

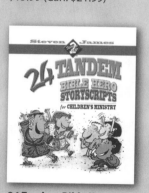